Personality Disorder

Managing Your Emotions and Improving Your Relationships

(A Specialist's Manual for Assume Command Reality With Regards to Antisocial)

Ricky Williams

Published By **Bella Frost**

Ricky Williams

All Rights Reserved

Personality Disorder: Managing Your Emotions and Improving Your Relationships (A Specialist's Manual for Assume Command Reality With Regards to Antisocial)

ISBN   978-1-998927-64-7

ISBN   978-1-998927-64-7

Legal & Disclaimer

The information contained in this book is not designed to replace or take the place of any form of medicine or professional medical advice. The information in this book has been provided for educational & entertainment purposes only.

The information contained in this book has been compiled from sources deemed reliable, and it is accurate to the best of the Author's knowledge; however, the Author cannot guarantee its accuracy and validity and cannot be held liable for any errors or omissions. Changes are periodically made to this book. You must consult your doctor or get professional medical advice before using any of the suggested remedies, techniques, or information in this book.

Table Of Contents

Chapter 1: What Is Antisocial Personality Disorder? 1

Chapter 2: The Five Subtypes Of Antisocial Personality Disorder 12

Chapter 3: Risk-Taking Antisocial Personality Disorder Subtype................. 19

Chapter 4: What Causes Antisocial Personality Disorder?............................. 29

Chapter 5: Five Common Therapy Methods For Antisocial Personality Disorder 55

Chapter 6: How To Overcome Antisocial Personality Disorder 77

Chapter 7: How To Find Your Escape 86

Chapter 8: Schizoid Personality Disorder 93

Chapter 9: Schizotypal Personality Disorder 97

Chapter 10: Schizophreniform Disorder 101

Chapter 11: Schizoaffective Disorder ... 105

Chapter 12: Depressive Disorders 109

Chapter 13: The Brief Psychotic Disorder 139

Chapter 14: Postpartum Disorder 144

Chapter 15: Borderline Personality Disorder 155

Chapter 16: What Is A Narcissist? 164

Chapter 17: How To Identify A Narcissist 169

Chapter 18: Living With A Narcissist..... 175

Chapter 19: Narcissists As Parents 181

Chapter 1: What is Antisocial Personality Disorder?

Antisocial Personality Disorder (ASPD) is someone disease that stops an man or woman from appealing with society in a regular way. Individuals with Antisocial Personality Disorder are normally not capable of come to be reliable people of society as their illness hinders their ability to meaningfully take part in family, corporation, or educational opportunities. The purpose for this hassle is due to their nature normally categorized as showing immoderate stages of self-significance, blatant push aside for others' rights, and a marked tendency to show off callous, cynical attitudes toward others. These humans are also more likely to interact in amoral behavior this is unacceptable with the useful resource of societal necessities.

To understand a sickness including Antisocial Personality Disorder, one need to in fact recognize the individual identified. This affords a trouble in phrases of desired take a look at, as it is not possible to sincerely preserve near and recognize some other man or woman whom you've got got in no way met in advance than. However, there are, in fashionable, some trends and commonalities that permit for a base statistics of those with Antisocial Personality Disorder, which offers a researcher notion into how this sickness develops.

Those who are recognized with Antisocial Personality Disorder normally will be inclined to share a very narcissistic view of themselves. These humans aren't modest human beings, however instead, accept as actual with themselves to be above others in essentially every elegance for which they area rate. If they'll or do extensively identified their lack in any location, which includes teachers, seems, or musical facts, for example, they'll have a correspondingly low evaluation of that location. Areas wherein they excel, they will location an emphasis on in phrases of usual importance even as concerning someone's 'rate'. This safeguards their excessive opinion of themselves, that may be a critical difficulty of their individual. Ironically, this narcissistic mind-set regularly covers a lack of self-self assurance, and those human beings also can have underlying self-esteem problems that need to be addressed.

In addition to their pretty narcissistic perspectives, the ones people are often specifically manipulative. While they do no longer see a outstanding deal of intrinsic price in others, they do see the greater tangible advantages that others can offer, and they'll now not hesitate to take benefit of others that allows you to make sure their very non-public comfort or improvement. With this motivation, a number of humans with delinquent personalities can, upon event, display massive knowledge in manipulating others for their personal abilities. This manipulation can also encompass a few diploma of attraction, which in flip can also reason others to doubt the authentic evaluation of Antisocial Personality Disorder.

However, this attraction isn't always some thing greater than a ground layer they produced via bloodless calculability to ensure their private status and does not communicate of the underlying motives or thoughts of the individual. When the purpose of their attraction has misplaced their usability, they may display the same blatant disregard for that person and their emotions as they do toward others.

This mind-set is a herbal barrier towards forming close, significant relationships with others. Therefore, further to their incapability to engage with others in a ordinary style, people with Antisocial Personality Disorder are also regularly remoted in the social stratum. This isolation hampers and, in massive diploma, prevents them from growing regular, healthful friendships. This lack of friendship throughout important years serves as a double-edged sword. While human beings with Antisocial Personality Disorder already warfare to realize the idea of "empathy", they're concurrently isolated from their buddies. This often reinforces their horrible perspectives in the direction of others.

These views normally turn out to be prominent at a few degree inside the teenage or younger character years. Because that may be a important time frame for person improvement, parents which are starting to enlarge antisocial conduct at some point of this period might also moreover go through extreme repercussions in terms of social popularity and future possibilities. For instance, teenagers who're beginning to make bigger Antisocial Personality Disorder may additionally alienate their buddies, ensuing of their very very own social isolation. This isolation also can serve as a contributing problem to horrific conduct, on the aspect of skipping magnificence or maybe taking trouble in more extreme unstable sports activities activities, which incorporates eating alcohol or taking drugs. These behaviors should have an apparent horrible effect on their ability to hold grades or make useful lifestyles picks, which includes making equipped for university. It is, therefore, common for humans with antisocial personalities to emerge as immoderate-college dropouts with the corresponding increased threat for horrible destiny life memories.

For human beings of this nature, adulthood, as diagnosed via way of the general population, can be some component they struggle with. Rather than behaving as calm, rational adults, those humans generally experience a 'stall-out' of their emotional boom, which impairs their capability to make responsible choices. While accepting responsibility on your very own conduct and acknowledging personal errors are important developments of maturity and maturity, those with Antisocial Personality Disorder are incapable of doing so. This loss of maturity results in improved impulsivity, a loss of forethought in choice making, and immoderate stages of selfishness.

Moreover, those awful attributes have an impact on greater than the people' mindset toward educational or career possibilities. In the non-public realm, people with Antisocial Personality Disorder go through quite various excessive setbacks. While every dating they've got is suffering from their disorder, their relationships with a romantic or sexual nature are greater brazenly affected. Individuals with Antisocial Personality Disorder are regularly mainly manipulative in the ones relationships. They can also moreover moreover turn out to be very exploitive in their partners, whilst their private behaviors are in all likelihood to be usually irresponsible. These human beings are frequently sexually promiscuous and can start showing sexual conduct at a reasonably younger age. In line with this, people with Antisocial Personality Disorder regularly dedicate infidelity in opposition to their friends, that could cause divorce. These people are also regarded to continuously and regularly lie to their associate and engage in dangerous sexual practices. Having sexual relationships with strangers, venture illicit affairs, and one in all a kind in addition troubling behaviors of similar nature are tendencies often located from people with ASPD.

While the impact in their Antisocial Personality Disorder is most effortlessly seen in their romantic relationships, they'll be no longer the best relationships affected. Relationships with mother and father, youngsters, and siblings are, likewise affected in a totally bad way and can reason tremendous tiers of strain on the general own family form. The inherently egocentric nature of those with Antisocial Personality Disorder, coupled with a high degree of immaturity and impulsivity make a achievement, responsible parenting a tough challenge. Caring for a kid calls for a diploma of sensitivity, forethought and selflessness that people with Antisocial Personality Disorder do not have. In addition, a infant is possibly to be visible as a burden through those with Antisocial Personality Disorder besides, or till, that toddler can offer them with a few shape of praise for their efforts.

Likewise, human beings with Antisocial Personality Disorder are maximum probably to be manipulative of their mother and father and might reason massive stress on their dating with them. As formerly cited, people with Antisocial Personality Disorder are frequently appreciably immature and they may depend heavily on their dad and mom' assist even via their person years. Their relationships with their siblings are also possibly to be negatively tormented by resentment and jealously that they experience. This terrible relationship is in all likelihood to be reinforced via the siblings who will often resent the individual with ASPD for inflicting such stress on their family unit, and the man or woman with ASPD will resent his or her siblings. It is, consequently, no marvel that circle of relatives relationships, which include a member with Antisocial Personality Disorder, are regularly particularly dysfunctional. It is crucial to observe, however, that at the same time as the family of these with Antisocial Personality Disorder is often dysfunctional, the own family unit can also play a vital feature in the remedy and a achievement manage of the affected individual's sickness. People with ASPD are not probably to have buddies outside the own family. Therefore, the exceptional deliver of resource they often get keep of is thru their own family.

This also can moreover appear like a harsh critique of these with Antisocial Personality Disorder however what is critical to recollect right here is that, as with each contamination, people will fall right into a continuum of those developments. Those who are more drastically affected by this ailment are likely to be greater manipulative, selfish, and narcissistic than their lots lots much less-affected contrary numbers. Likewise, no longer each affected individual will display the identical set of behaviors as others. Some people might also even come to be greater capable mother and father (despite the truth that being termed 'herbal' isn't going) than others. Due to those versions, Theodore Milton has diagnosed 5 subtypes of Antisocial Personality Disorder. These subtypes are called Malevolent Antisocial, Covetous Antisocial, Risk-Taking Antisocial, Reputation-Defending Antisocial, and Nomadic Antisocial.

Chapter 2: The five Subtypes of Antisocial Personality Disorder

Theodore Millon is a stated American psychologist who turn out to be most acknowledged for his art work on character sickness subtypes. He is credited with identifying subtypes for a couple of persona disorders, which includes Schizoid Personality Disorder, Obsessive-Compulsive Personality Disorder, Narcissistic Personality Disorder, and of direction, Antisocial Personality Disorder. There are five subtypes that Millon recognized for Antisocial Personality Disorder. Each subtype has its very very own traits and demanding situations for the affected person, and patients need to keep in mind their very personal subtype whilst searching for treatment or analysis.

Malevolent Antisocial Personality Subtype

Those who fall into the malevolent subtype of Antisocial Personality Disorder can be idea of as your 'conventional villain'. This is not to mention that those humans associated with this subtype are 'evil' however, as an alternative, humans belonging to the malevolent subtype will be inclined to expose abilities and inclinations that shows the historical portrayal of villainous characters. These humans are commonly brutal, vicious humans. This can be the direct end stop end result of the character's lack of ability to enjoy empathy from the ones round them. But regardless of the cause, they're regularly exceedingly harsh toward others. This brutality is not simplest displayed through verbal or social mediums, but may reflect in direct physical assaults devoted by means of the affected man or woman.

This is mainly actual if the affected man or woman feels that they've been wronged in any manner. When they feel that their values and thoughts are beneath attack, they'll reply with vicious strain. Revenge is an concept that holds exceptional enchantment for the ones inside the malevolent subtype and that they maintain no compunction about carrying out acts to advantage this intention. Moreover, the ones within the malevolent subtype aren't going to be constrained of their desires by means of using a very superior judgment of proper and wrong.

While now not diagnosed as a diagnosable contamination thru wider intellectual circles, in extra crook justice oriented settings, these human beings are regularly classified as either sociopaths or psychopaths. There is a moderate difference most of the 2, which renders some conflict in expert circles over the class of those people. However, it's miles sufficient to say that the ones people be troubled through a excessive abnormality within the region of experience of proper and incorrect, to the amount that the man or woman may be regarded as though it'd lack a experience of right and incorrect in any respect. This impairment of the texture of right and incorrect lets in the malevolent subtype individual to take actions that others can also find out untenable. Paired with the general need for revenge displayed via using the usage of those individuals, the ones on this subtype can take drastic, malicious actions in opposition to others which could bring about essential damage.

Moreover, the malevolent delinquent man or woman anticipates betrayal from others. This expectation leads the affected individual to count on a defensive position previous to an attack, ensuing inside the affected character taking preemptive motion. In actual worldwide phrases, the ones in this subtype frequently attack others before they themselves are attacked that lets in you to guard themselves. Furthermore, rather than sense a few semblance of remorse or regret for their moves, human beings on this subtype are probably to reveal a callous, belligerent mind-set with reference to their personal behavior. To this affected person, the maximum crucial character is, in fact, himself or herself. Therefore, any motion taken to protect themselves, or to punish the ones who've harmed them in any fashion, is perfectly suitable behavior. Instead of believing themselves to be within the wrong, they firmly take delivery of as authentic with that their personal movements are each justifiable and inexpensive.

Covetous Antisocial Personality Disorder Subtype

It can also come as no surprise that one of the defining characteristics of the covetous subtype of Antisocial Personality Disorder is a marked penchant for greed. It may be stated that anybody are greedy in some thing, and that is likely right. However, for the ones people who fall into the covetous subtype, their greed extends past normal bounds and affects each how they view the sector and their relationships with others. The desires and dreams of those people come to be an essential a part of their persona and they're pushed to gain these things regardless of price or previous possession.

In truth, the covetous delinquent will quality want some factor extra if it's miles denied them, or if ownership has already been installation thru way of some other. For the ones people, a large a part of their delight in expertise their goals and dreams isn't always lots as having, but in taking. This gives numerous issues for the affected man or woman with regards to a social placing. In a few instances, this choice may additionally lead to vital and probable unlawful moves that can have severe repercussions. In addition, it is obvious that this tendency to need what others have will reason some measure of friction with individuals who declare earlier ownership. Therefore this tendency may additionally moreover lead now not simplest to trouble with criminal government, but also with friends, pals, and others.

Moreover, those humans experience intentionally denied with the useful resource of others. For those human beings, taking what others have is a degree they deem every essential and appropriate. This is basically due to the truth they do now not take delivery of as true with that others will freely deliver what they accept as true with they deserve.

Moreover, the ones people will be predisposed to truely receive as real with that they deserve pretty masses. Paired with their often irresponsible, selfish, and albeit slothful conduct, earning what they agree with they deserve is a difficult mission for the ones human beings. The disparity amongst what they understand they deserve and what they're able to earning for themselves is virtually too notable generally. This can reason resentment within the direction of others of behalf of the patient, while also reaffirming their 'If I want it, i'll take it' thoughts-set.

Chapter 3: Risk-Taking Antisocial Personality Disorder Subtype

The risk-taking subtype of Antisocial Personality Disorder is especially thrilling. Persons below the hazard-taking subtype are not characterised with the resource of intrinsic dispositions, together with greed or cruelty, however are as an alternative stated for their brash behavior. Perhaps because of the lack of everyday maturity advanced, those in this subtype are diagnosed for his or her reckless moves, most significantly the ones actions that pose big risks to their safety and others'. This also can be because of the affected man or woman's lack of impulse manage, a substantially significant trait of these with antisocial individual sickness.

This lack of impulse manage also can additionally vary depending at the character. For the ones of the covetous subtype, as an example, this loss of impulse manipulate may moreover take the shape of theft. Those inside the malevolent subtype, however, may additionally additionally take area this trait by using striking others in anger. However, for the risk-taking subtype, this lack of manipulate famous itself in risky and impetuous actions, such as riding below the have an effect on, rushing, and intense sports activities sports sports.

This subtype is ruled through an audacious character type that performs nicely in movies however in actual-existence constitutes severe hazard. Though they are high-quality stated for his or her reckless conduct, the ones human beings but have the narcissistic tendencies that Antisocial Personality Disorder is associated with. These tendencies, mixed with their ambitious individual, can certainly alienate others. This subtype is, but, possibly the least likely to honestly estrange themselves from others. While the terrible tendencies of Antisocial Personality Disorder are although present, their popularity on excessive-risk behaviors and coffee suggests of appeal can create a certain attraction to others.

This subtype of Antisocial Personality Disorder consists of histrionic talents, this means that they frequently display hobby-looking for behaviors and extreme emotionality. Consistent with the opposite subtypes of Antisocial Personality Disorder, the risk-taking character does sense a enjoy of superiority over others. However, the ones human beings need to be the focal point of these round them, and are regularly ardent of their pursuit of interest. These are the standout people – assume well-known, well-known people who simultaneously need the adoration of others whilst believing the ones identical people aren't as genuine as them.

It may also moreover seem that that is a maximum pleasant form for antisocial behavior to take, and in a few regard one might be accurate. However, there are negative elements to this subtype that should no longer be unnoticed. For example, even as their unstable antics and dramatic fashion could probable engender a few shape of awe from others, those humans are not going to have actual, meaningful relationships. They are not immune from the lousy elements of Antisocial Personality Disorder, which makes them often have issue organising and preserving relationships. They are particularly narcissistic and effortlessly insulted, and the horrible opinions of those spherical them may also significantly have an effect on their happiness. It is consequently important to recollect that, at the same time as the horrible facets of different subtypes can be more right away maximum essential, the chance-taking subtype moreover has horrible attributes.

Reputation-Defending Antisocial Personality Disorder Subtype

The reputation-protective subtype of Antisocial Personality Disorder is maximum successfully named. To individuals of this subtype, their recognition acts as a form of armor. For them, their popularity is a few thing that establishes their superiority over others, while on the equal time prevents them from being harmed by way of others. These humans need others to appearance them as a outstanding character, as a person who has no flaws to make the most or weak spot to take gain of.

By necessity, the person format of this recognition will vary due to the conditions of the man or woman involved. For instance, a Nineteen Fifties technology woman with this subtype may additionally want others to appearance her due to the fact the extremely good housewife. She ought to want no rumors approximately her own family, cover a few element that didn't in shape her 'great' photo, and use this recognition to ruthlessly choose her contemporaries. This reputation may take a highly one-of-a-type shape for a current woman, who may want to be seen because the right businesswoman. Her reputation can be based totally on her ruthlessness and not unusual sense, her bloodless practicality, or her decreasing intelligence. She might want to guard her recognition in competition to rumors of her softness, that being a girl has impacted her functionality to influence, or that she has allowed her emotions control her movements.

The issue of these examples isn't to problem out the stereotypes of diverse eras however to as an alternative emphasize that the time and location wherein people below the popularity-defensive subtype discover themselves plays a huge feature in the form of popularity they want to installation. What will no longer trade based totally totally on the ones outside elements is they want to be seen as 'best' with the aid of way of their contemporaries. Moreover, in addition to being visible as 'perfect' with the resource of the use of others, those humans need to be visible as 'unbreakable' or 'untouchable' within the eyes of others. Though this is of direction a façade, human beings of this subtype use that façade to guard them and to discourage assaults from outside sports in the direction of them. Due to this, they region a excessive diploma of importance on appearance and end up steadfast at the same time as their role is threatened.

In the same manner, the ones of this subtype are tenacious even as protecting their reputation. They are probable to take excessive motion when they experience that their popularity is being threatened by means of manner of the use of others and will haven't any trouble resorting to drastic measures to make sure their very very own fulfillment. For those patients, their recognition is a treasured middle thing of their identity. While their moves may additionally furthermore seem exaggerated to others, the recognition-protecting subtype are absolutely protective a important detail of themselves. Likewise, those people reply to threats to their reputation much like how others ought to probably reply while their honor or ethics are puzzled or threatened.

Nomadic Antisocial Personality Disorder Subtype

The nomadic delinquent individual is someone who's regularly located at the peripheral of society. One may also need to even name them the 'forgotten' in contemporary society. They are characterized with the useful resource of gypsy-like dispositions, such that they no longer often set up an area for themselves among society. Rather, they wander within the route of their existence, in no way without a doubt finding a place that fits them sufficient to stay. This drifting is going past their bodily location – they flow from activity to method, dating to relationship, never really cementing themselves to every person or a few aspect.

They are the dropouts and misfits, who enjoy as despite the fact that they are society leftovers. Often this will lead those humans to emerge as vagrants, and they will frequently enjoy both poverty and homelessness. Though others may additionally region the blame for this mostly on the people' movements, the affected person will regularly revel in as although they'll be 'jinxed'. These humans regularly have higher stages of self-pity. They won't discover price in exerting a exquisite deal attempt as they consider that no matter the attempt they installed they may not acquire a outstanding final consequences.

The nomadic subtype has competencies of each the avoidant and schizoid personalities. This is a heavy aggregate that, as quickly as paired with the herbal capabilities of Antisocial Personality Disorder, evidently produces awful consequences. The avoidant abilities that gift themselves within the nomadic subtype can be answerable for the tendency of the patient to move on in desire to war to set up themselves in a given feature. This itinerant behavior has maximum crucial drawbacks for the affected man or woman. First, they are not capable of create any real bond with others. This loss of bond with others limits the affected individual's sources, in each their bodily and emotional functionality. Whereas others are able to depend on pals and own family in times of want, their avoidant nature ensures that the nomadic antisocial is isolated. Secondly, their escapist dispositions prevent the patient from taking motion to cope with their underlying issues, together with their horrible attitude.

Their schizoid function reinforces the issues these people face in putting in place bonds or going via their very very own shortcomings. A schizoid trait refers to an character's problem in setting up relationships with others, particularly due to their loss of ability to each unique or respond to feelings. This loss of emotion and apparent detachment outcomes to schizoid capabilities regularly taking the placement of the 'loner' who's without buddies and looks no longer to want any. However, as it has already been hooked up, a relationship with others is vital for each monetary and intellectual health. The lack of these bonds promotes the conditions for the ones of the nomadic subtype to come to be isolated from society and revel in all of the problems that include that isolation.

Chapter 4: What Causes Antisocial Personality Disorder?

Antisocial Personality Disorder, like maximum personality troubles, is idea to be the result of a aggregate of factors. These elements are to be had in exquisite regards: genetic or natural factors, which embody risk factors, collectively with hereditary factors, chemical or hormonal imbalances, or early thoughts harm and environmental factors, which embody domestic lifestyles, socialization, gaining knowledge of, and lots of others. The extra those hazard factors are gift for a given character, the extra the hazard that he or she might be capable of expand Antisocial Personality Disorder. However, this does not suggest that every one individuals who have some or maybe all of these chance elements observed in them will, in reality, develop Antisocial Personality Disorder. Diagnosis must be done thru a expert and have to be primarily based on conduct, not chance factors.

Biological Factors

Humans are complicated beings. There are such numerous minute records which is probably essential to the steadiness of an character that setting apart a single factor in abnormal improvement is a hard, if now not not possible, challenge. For this reason, there are various special theories on which natural factors increase an character's risk for growing Antisocial Personality Disorder. Moreover, numerous precise theories have a few evidence of their veracity. Therefore, it's far pretty probably that extra than the form of theories are correct and that the more the aggregate of these elements, the more likely an individual is to expand Antisocial Personality Disorder.

One of the herbal theories for Antisocial Personality Disorder is that it is a give up result of an normal development of the hectic device. The apprehensive machine is a community of cells and fibers that transmit nerve impulses (thoughts and actions) from one part of the body to each different. Ultimately, the worried device controls our mind and movements. If an man or woman has an abnormality in their concerned device, this abnormality can reason excessive issues for that person. Identifying an abnormality in the concerned device can be a tough task. Learning disorders, regular prolonged-time period bedwetting, and hyperactivity are all feasible signs and symptoms of an abnormality inside the concerned system. If an person indicates those attributes, there might be an extended chance for that person to additionally model antisocial behavior.

Another organic chance detail for Antisocial Personality Disorder is maternal smoking at some point of being pregnant. Scientists agree with that once a mom smokes for the duration of being pregnant, the oxygen supplied to the fetus is impaired. This loss of oxygen also can bring about minor varieties of mind damage to the unborn toddler. While this harm might not be proper away observable or have an impact at the physical fitness of the kid (notwithstanding the truth that precise results of prenatal smoking without a doubt do), later in development, this damage would possibly in all likelihood ultimately have a large effect. Studies showed that those humans whose mother smoked at the equal time as pregnant are much more likely to show off delinquent behavior, have interaction in antisocial conduct, and feature issues with behavior.

Sensory input is likewise related to Antisocial Personality Disorder. There is proof that people who require a greater quantity of sensory input are at risk of Antisocial Personality Disorder. Sensory input refers to a person's capacity to prepare and use the records relayed to them via their senses. In people with a low herbal sensory input, there can be a risk that they will take part in extra risky sports sports to raise their arousal stages, thereby pleasing their need for extended sensory input. The proof that antisocial patients have low resting coronary heart costs as well as low pores and skin conductance helps this concept. Brain scans have moreover validated that the ones who've antisocial character ailment have decrease degrees on tremendous thoughts measures, reinforcing the concept that sensory input may additionally have an effect at the delinquent behavior of the patient.

Aside from this sensory enter, uncommon mind function has moreover been related to delinquent conduct. This concept is based definitely at the knowledge that the temporal lobes and prefrontal cortex manipulate each temper and conduct. If those regions of the thoughts are functioning improperly, or had been damaged to 3 diploma, delinquent conduct may additionally additionally moreover give up result. Likewise, serotonin is likewise believed to be a functionality cause of Antisocial Personality Disorder. Serotonin is a neurotransmitter, which permits relay symptoms within the mind. If the tiers of serotonin are imbalanced, temper and concept methods may be affected. For this reason, serotonin imbalances had been related to depression, similarly to Antisocial Personality Disorder.

There is likewise the risk that Antisocial Personality Disorder may be inherited through a right away hereditary link. This is evidenced via the big popularity that folks that are recognized with Antisocial Personality Disorder are frequently the kids of delinquent human beings themselves. This is a hyperlink that might normally be followed in some unspecified time in the future of generations, further to for the duration of familial wooden, to installation a pattern of a right away hereditary cause.

Environment Factors

Just as genetic or organic factors play a large role in figuring out the possibilities of developing Antisocial Personality Disorder; environmental elements additionally may be contributing factors. The social environment begins offevolved with the mother and father, so it is no marvel that children with antisocial mother and father are more likely to be antisocial themselves. Antisocial parents are not probably an amazing manner to provide a strong domestic surroundings, or offer the critical emotional assist for a kid to increase commonly. In the absence of this stability, and coupled with the limited emotional comments they get maintain of, youngsters also can find out techniques to reveal antisocial behavior themselves. Though, of direction, some may additionally moreover additionally argue that that may be a component for a hereditary link to delinquent behavior as nicely.

A hyperlink has been set up a number of the conduct of dad and mom and the conduct of their kids. For example, a big study discovered a correlation the various popularity of antisocial boys and alcoholic dad and mom. Parents of antisocial boys have been determined to be much more likely to have criminal pasts and inclinations, and there is often a presence of divorce or separation. The absence of a determine is a particularly excessive hazard problem for children to boom Antisocial Personality Disorder. The principle to offer an motive of this hyperlink is that the dearth of a parental bond prevents the child from feeling steady in a social scenario. Isolated from this important bond, the child learns to isolate him or herself from others as properly.

This is likewise believed due to the fact the purpose for the prolonged chance for antisocial conduct among followed kids. Children for adoption are regularly moved from domestic to home prior to being completely positioned with a circle of relatives. This motion from home to domestic frequently takes vicinity within the direction of a essential period in a baby's development, that may have excessive repercussions on the kid's psyche. The incapacity to form an extended-term bond in the direction of this period, alongside aspect a experience of isolation and abandonment, can cause the child to end up withdrawn from all the ones round them. The last quit end result of this form of scenario is the development of antisocial behavior, likely essential to Antisocial Personality Disorder later on. While the evaluation of Antisocial Personality Disorder can most effective be made after a person reaches 18 years vintage, youngsters who are seen to be at danger for the improvement of this illness and given preemptive care might also additionally lessen, or maybe remove, the terrible outcomes of this sickness.

Overall, the development of Antisocial Personality Disorder might be because of a convergence of a couple of chance factors. Being genetically predisposed or biologically vulnerable to this individual disorder genuinely plays a big detail in whether or now not someone develops an delinquent character. However, it is unusual for those factors on my own to offer Antisocial Personality Disorder. Oftentimes, there may be a genetic predisposition this is brought on with the useful resource of an environmental element, which eventually ends up to the sickness. However, the intellectual community has installed no formal reason of Antisocial Personality Disorder. This is, in element, due to the trouble of distinguishing what styles of danger factors for Antisocial Personality Disorder are causation elements and which elements are correlation factors. Causation factors are elements which have an instantaneous impact on the development of a disorder or situation. Correlation elements speak over with elements that may be present simultaneously with a illness however are impartial of the disorder. In the case of Antisocial Personality Disorder, figuring out what's a cause and what is a correlation element to the contamination is complex with the useful resource of the use of the confined viable studies techniques, the late time period analysis, and the intricacy of the elements themselves.

The 9 Most Common Symptoms of Antisocial Personality Disorder

1. Disregard for Right or Wrong

Patients with Antisocial Personality Disorder regularly disregard society's idea of 'proper' or 'wrong' behavior. This is the result of elements of the delinquent personality- the dearth of a social bond, and a narcissistic outlook. Those with Antisocial Personality Disorder frequently fail to set up strong bonds with the rest of society, and so, they will be not positive by way of the use of the social mores society makes use of to keep peace and harmony. For instance, even if there aren't any formal pointers in a tough and fast, unspoken suggestions will exist. These regulations serve to preserve the organisation homogenous and enhance the sturdy bond maximum of the people that compose the employer. Breaking the ones hints can also moreover result in isolation or alienation from the ones human beings, which serves as a motivator to conform with installed policies. Those with Antisocial Personality Disorder lack the ones bonds and, for this reason aren't hampered with the aid of way of a want to be preferred or contemporary via others, liberating them from the need to act 'effectively'. This freedom is compounded by using manner of using the narcissistic mind-set of these people. Not simplest are they loose from emotional motivation to do the 'right' factor, furthermore they consider themselves to be above others. This creates a state of affairs wherein the ones sufferers enjoy they may be above the policies. This trait moreover encourages the affected individual to location their personal goals and troubles above the ones of others, thereby number one the affected person to make the awesome choice for his or her pastimes, instead of the morally or socially applicable choice.

2. Manipulating Others

Patients with Antisocial Personality Disorder are noted for their capability and willingness to control others. The purpose for this manipulation can also moreover additionally range thru person or via manner of scenario, and may be for either personal benefit or surely because they enjoy doing so. In preferred, those people undergo in thoughts that they'll be above others. Therefore, they have got little compunction approximately manipulating one-of-a-kind 'lesser' humans for his or her personal pride. Some of those people can also moreover additionally even justify their manipulation internally, excusing their conduct because of the truth 'it acquired't harm everyone' or 'it doesn't bear in mind'. Others may be so isolated from the social norm that they do no longer feel the want for this justification. They do not forget that they're handiest doing what they want and the obligation lies with the celebration who's permitting themselves to be manipulated.

This form of manipulation also can range as nicely. Oftentimes, the shape of manipulation the patient chooses can be decided on primarily based totally on what they receive as true with has the awesome danger of success. In a few instances, this can require lying. Those with Antisocial Personality Disorder are mentioned to be common liars to a few diploma. If the affected character believes that mendacity to a person will garner the response they want, they'll be no longer probably to hesitate to do so. However, in instances in which lying isn't a opportunity, the ones human beings can and could inn to the use of their attraction to govern others. These human beings are pretty foxy and they may be frequently able to win over others, imparting themselves virtually as another form of person. This photo is used to manipulate the alternative birthday celebration till this type of time at the same time as the affected man or woman not desires them. At that point, they will frequently stop their charade of attraction or stop contact completely with the opportunity man or woman.

Three.   Extreme Egocentrism

Those who are selfish are involved first and fundamental with their very very own issues. They are 'me' human beings, centered on their non-public goals, needs, and desires. For the affected man or woman with Antisocial Personality Disorder, this preoccupation with the self is even more outstanding. The primary precedence they've got is their own self-improvement. To reap their dreams, they may hotel to any manner, which include mendacity, dishonest, stealing... none of it subjects, as long as they gain from their moves. While it could seem counterintuitive, this severe reputation on their very personal dreams acts as a stumbling block to their personal personal improvement, their relationships with others, and ultimately, their very private achievement in existence. Individuals cannot succeed with out the assist of others, and constantly placing your own needs and wants above those of others is not going to inspire them to offer help on the same time because the time comes.

Altruistic behavior, or self-sacrificing for the advantage of others, is something people with Antisocial Personality Disorder cannot understand. The quality way to understand this trait of the antisocial character is to recognize that to the affected man or woman with Antisocial Personality Disorder, existence is a war and every interplay they have got with others is regarded as though it would be a battle. In this 'struggle' the simplest man or woman the antisocial person is stopping for is himself or herself. Seen on this way, it's far less complex to recognize the mentality of the Antisocial Personality Disorder patient.

Four.   Recurring Issues with the Law

The affected individual with Antisocial Personality Disorder has numerous inclinations which make her or him much more likely to return returned into contact with law enforcement in a awful way. To start with, humans with Antisocial Personality Disorder have a trouble with authority figures of any type. This starts with their parents, remains genuine with instructors, and in the end results in law enforcement. These people virtually do now not have a high-quality deal of tolerance or recognize for the tips of others, even if the 'others' are police or society in famous. They are consequently more likely to interrupt the regulation, particularly in extra petty methods consisting of shoplifting or rushing.

While such petty crimes might be more time-commemorated among human beings with ASPD, they will be virtually at danger to have interaction in greater severe crime as nicely, especially infant abuse or neglect, and extra competitive crimes, which incorporates attack or battery. These movements can lead those people to the eye of the police. As such, they regularly have lengthy rap sheets of crook hobby. It is thrilling to word that the ones humans are also much more likely to face up to arrest. This might be the stop end result of the convergence in their truly competitive behavior paired with their loss of admire for authority figures. Unfortunately, this will frequently compound their difficulties with regulation enforcement and may bring about a more excessive charge and sentence.

5. Repeated Violations of Others Rights

The rights of others aren't of a bargain trouble to people with Antisocial Personality

Disorder. In all honesty, those sufferers have a blatant disregard for the rights of others and feature simply no compunction about violating the ones rights. 'Rights' speak to the crucial freedom of a person that is diagnosed through way of society. These rights can encompass the entirety from the most primary freedoms, which encompass making an knowledgeable choice, to lifestyles-changing factors which embody the right of duplicate. This is pretty a difficult concern be counted and may display tough to apprehend inside the starting. To benefit a better knowledge, it is splendid to peer the ones violations in context.

For example, the proper to manipulate your potential to have a toddler, and the right to determine whether or not or no longer or not you need a toddler, is a essential human right. However, if someone with Antisocial Personality Disorder had a honestly one in every of a type opinion approximately whether or not or now not to or not to have a little one, they will now not hesitate to make that choice truely thru the use of themselves, with out regard to their companion's rights at the challenge. For instance, if a woman affected character with Antisocial Personality Disorder believed that having a infant should in all likelihood beautify (or preserve, depending on the country of the relationship) her dating she may lie to her companion and make a deliberate try and get pregnant. In this example, she disregards the proper of her accomplice to decide whether or not or now not he would like to have a baby. Likewise, the reverse also can be right. If a male affected individual believes that having a toddler would possibly cement his courting with a girl, he can also lie or manage sports to impregnate his accomplice. This can be an excessive example, but the popular essence is the same. These human beings regard their very own desires and rights because of the truth the high-quality important element in you make a decision, and they'll again and again violate the rights of others to be able to acquire their personal desires.

6. Child Abuse or Neglect

It is hard for loads to understand how someone with Antisocial Personality Disorder dad and mom their child, or extra as it must be, fails to perform that. The first component one have to recognize about antisocial parents is the way they view their little one. In many instances, humans with Antisocial Personality Disorder grow to be parents out of properly judgment or as an twist of destiny. These human beings are, for lack of a better time period, very bloodless people. They will now not hesitate to deliver a little one for their egocentric motives. However, while the purpose for the child disappears – or as fast as the child has fulfilled its reason – the delinquent decide frequently sees the child as a burden as opposed to a gift. The patient may emerge as pregnant (or impregnate some one of a kind) via the use of twist of fate, and terminating or adopting the child might not be an possibility. In this case, the figure ought to in all likelihood experience that the child is a burden that drains belongings from their most essential character – themselves.

Children require extraordinary try, persistence, and love from their parents. However, patients with Antisocial Personality Disorder do not have the ones objects to provide. Thus, every little one abuse and toddler forget regularly arise on the equal time as the decide in query has Antisocial Personality Disorder. Children of those humans may be physically or mentally abused, becoming the purpose in their decide's frustrations. They can also be not noted because of the reality the number one difficulty as people with ASPD most effective keep in thoughts themselves number one problem number one. Everyone else, even his or her private little one, will come 2d. This can bring about malnourishment, lack of health, uncleanliness, and extra. Forming a bond with the determine with ASPD is, undeniably, difficult to boom and this, in turn, can propagate the cycle, as the child of the affected man or woman is also possibly to increase Antisocial Personality Disorder.

7. Extreme Negative Emotions

Everyone has a terrible day from time to time, and anybody reports intervals of bad feelings. People may be irritable and they might do topics all of a unexpected, which they may remorse later. These are regular occurrences and do now not commonly present overly dramatic issues in an regular individual's life. However, humans with Antisocial Personality Disorder are in no way 'popular'. These individuals will regularly revel in excessive degrees of terrible, risky emotions that pose a right away chance to their private and others' intellectual stability. These horrible emotions encompass hostility, impulsiveness and agitation, and can virtually bring about extreme situations. Individuals who experience the ones feelings of their whole intensity are probable to make huge errors and horrible alternatives, which result to excessive repercussions. For instance, they will create warfare with others or have interaction in self-damage because of the ones negative feelings.

Violence, aggression and irritability also are commonplace signs of Antisocial Personality Disorder. These dangerous feelings could have important results, including bodily violence. Combined with their impulsive nature and natural immaturity, their competitive conduct can purpose them to intense hassle. These emotions are regularly the underlying motive for his or her commonplace encounters with law enforcement, which might probably negatively have an impact on non-public and industrial business company relationships. Overall, those feelings present a extreme problem for the affected man or woman with Antisocial Personality Disorder. Unless they hold close their feelings, it can grow to be a harmful element inside the affected person's lifestyles.

8. Lack of Empathy

Empathy is the functionality of an individual to understand every other individual, permitting an individual to take a look at a situation with a few different person's angle in thoughts. In an incorporated society, empathy is a crucial functionality, as it permits people to end up extra forgiving, information, and accepting of others. Unfortunately, empathy is an emotional device that human beings with Antisocial Personality Disorder nearly universally lack. This reasons numerous problems for the affected man or woman on the facet of the opposite problems due to the sickness. For example, this loss of empathy curtails the functionality of the affected character to experience remorse for his or her actions. Empathy can't be present without information; and in case you do no longer sympathize with each other character, there may be now not anything to forestall you from causing harm.

This loss of empathy at the equal time as combined with being selfish and narcissistic tendencies, create a totally self-targeted character, believing that they will be superior to anybody and not able to empathize with others. They are the correct specimen to emerge as tyrannical dictators or perhaps serial killers. This isn't to mention that all people who've Antisocial Personality Disorder are serial killers, or are 'evil'. This is without a doubt, unequivocally, not the case. However, it can't be denied that there may be nice preponderance in the ones infamous populations for Antisocial Personality Disorder to be conventional.

9. Dangerous Behavior

Maturity, practicality, and rationality are the skills assisting someone to make affordable choices. More importantly, they help prevent a person from making horrific choices. When the ones factors are lacking – imprudent choices can be made. These irresponsible alternatives regularly come within the form of dangerous behavior collectively with vehicle browsing, under the have an effect on of alcohol riding, texting on the same time as the use of, and many others. But the ones behaviors also can include tons much less obvious sorts of risky conduct, which include having unprotected intercourse with a stranger, assignment unlawful sports activities activities, or taking tablets.

Chapter 5: Five Common Therapy Methods for Antisocial Personality Disorder

Treatment for Antisocial Personality Disorder is a hard, complicated, and extended-term affair. Treatment is the most effective at the equal time as began out early or even because it starts offevolved to show up, ideally in early adolescents or children. Treatment at an early diploma is much more likely to have a excessive outstanding final effects. However, this illness isn't being diagnosed until the affected person reaches 18 years of age, early remedy options may not be an preference. This gives a trouble due to the fact older sufferers with Antisocial Personality Disorder are particularly now not going to are searching for remedy on their very non-public, and generally do not accept as actual with that remedy is vital the least bit. Though their illness can intrude with their lives and everyday happiness, sufferers aren't probably to recognize that reality and seldom discover fault with their very own behavior.

Considering this truth, it may frequently take a large amount of strive before people with this circumstance will are in search of treatment. Often, patients are required to are searching for remedy as a part of a courtroom-mandated order or as a part of their sentencing.

Treatment itself is not an smooth or speedy tool, regardless of what character chooses as a remedy possibility. Treatment have to generally be conducted on an extended-term basis and improvement in condition is associated with the affected person's open-mindedness and willingness to enhance. If a patient who has been coerced into looking for treatment (and that they often must be) is reluctant to change or refuses to admit they have got a trouble, the treatment approach can be useless or drawn-out. With that stated, there are numerous alternatives for parents that are willing to are searching for remedy.

1. Psychotherapy

The first of these options is psychotherapy, furthermore called 'talk-remedy' and seemed to be the conventional shape of treatment. It includes putting in place a courting among an authorized psychologist or psychiatrist and the affected man or woman, and using that relationship to help talk the patient through his or her disorder. Over time, the affected individual can apprehend and avoid the negative elements of their conditions and study best coping behaviors. Psychoanalytical treatment alternatives will now not commonly be successful with this situation. Practitioners ought to therefore attention on putting in place motivation and building connections among properly behaviors and splendid reinforcements. The key at the same time as treating Antisocial Personality Disorder is convincing the sufferers that they need and need to change the kinds of their conduct. If this is completed, some form of success can be executed. This treatment can be performed through man or woman, organisation or own family instructions. Even pals can take part inside the treatment session, so long as a expert practitioner is venture the session. There are not any dangerous factor effects to this treatment alternative.

However, the disadvantage to the psychotherapy treatment desire is that outcomes aren't assured. If sufferers refuse to look that they've a hassle and are unwilling to address the problem, the results won from psychotherapy may be non-existent. Moreover, talk remedy can take a large amount of time in advance than any gradual results are enormous. The extra intense the signs and signs and symptoms are the greater strive on the part of the affected man or woman is wanted to look improvement. If the signs and signs and symptoms and signs are severe enough, there might not be any excellent development the least bit.

2. Medications

Medication is each different remedy alternative for Antisocial Personality Disorder. However, there can be no specific medication for Antisocial Personality Disorder itself. Psychiatrists also can pick out to prescribe drug remedies that address the signs and symptoms of the illness or to deal with concurrent mental problems that exacerbate the affected man or woman's state of affairs. These drugs are commonly antipsychotics, antidepressants, or temper stabilizers. Medications together with serotonin uptake inhibitors (additionally known as ssris) can assist some sufferers with aggressive or depressed behaviors. These inhibitors encompass medicines which consist of Prozac or Zoloft, which can be regularly prescribed for pretty pretty a variety of person issues.

One gain of the medicine remedy is they may have a proper away effect at the patient. Aggression, impulsivity and hostility can all be without a doubt regulated with the resource of way of medicinal tablets whilst well prescribed. Another advantage is the benefit of remedy. Patients do now not should located forth a remarkable deal of strive for this remedy desire to take impact – even though they should at least take their medicinal pills frequently. Even if a affected character is mentally unwilling to exchange, as long as they take their remedy, a few enhancements can be made. This treatment alternative is likewise appreciably faster than psychotherapy, that could take an prolonged term. Medication, in evaluation, starts to take effect in a recollect of weeks if no longer days of starting treatment.

The advantages of drugs also can spark off many to pick out out this treatment method. However, there are a widespread range of drawbacks to this remedy approach that need to be taken into consideration. Most appreciably, there is no treatment that has been authorised with the aid of the Food and Drug Administration for the treatment of Antisocial Personality Disorder. This manner that, even as the drug treatments stated above can also have some effects on the signs and symptoms and signs and signs, the sickness itself is not cured through manner of those medicines. Stopping treatment will bring about a close to on the spot rebound of in advance signs and symptoms, and those signs and symptoms and signs and symptoms may additionally also be worse than earlier than the remedy started.

Additionally, medicinal pills have crucial side outcomes and risks that other remedy alternatives do no longer very very own. Zoloft, for instance, has severa awful feasible detail consequences which includes insomnia, diarrhea, nausea, elevated danger for suicide, fatigue, indigestion and similarly. It is likewise now not encouraged for women who are pregnant, which means that that a pregnant affected person can be compelled to forestall medication whilst gestating, probable undoing any earlier progress. Prozac has a comparable listing of functionality aspect results. Another downside of medicines is the functionality problem that arises whilst a affected person is on treatment for a few different situation. Medications do no longer usually interact properly with each unique, and taking certain medicine concurrently can bring about extreme issue outcomes. It won't be possible, for some sufferers to pick out this treatment desire if a preceding health situation requires them to take a treatment that would have interaction badly with the medication for their Antisocial Personality Disorder.

Three.   Behavioral Skills Lessons

A 1/three desire for the remedy of Antisocial Personality Disorder is for the affected man or woman to interact in behavioral skills education. These are education that teach people the manner to behave in a pleasant manner in wider society and set up tremendous hyperlinks among socially acceptable behaviors and self-blessings for the affected man or woman. This treatment opportunity is similar to that of psychotherapy, however there are some critical situations that separate the two treatments.

The maximum essential distinction amongst those remedies is the issuer of the remedy.

While there are numerous options at the same time as choosing education in behavioral talents like behavioral faculties, the patients do not need to are searching out treatment from a psychologist or psychiatrist. This is useful due to the reality the sufferers may be greater willing to paintings with their instructor and may be less on guard. Especially in times wherein the affected character is ordered to are seeking for remedy by way of the courts, they will be reluctant to speak in self notion to a therapist. Behavioral commands cast off this impediment in remedy. However, the shortage of a expert can also be a drawback, due to the fact the trainer might not be honestly certified to help these people. Another downside of the behavioral schooling is the constrained capability to assist the affected character.

While those training also can furthermore help the affected character find out how to expose off higher social behaviors, they do not cope with underlying causes and troubles of the affected individual. Dealing with complex issues together with the affected individual's anger and aggression also can be past the scope of behavioral instructions. For those reasons, it's miles quality if behavioral instructions are factors of an normal treatment plan, in preference to a sole direction of treatment.

4. Support Groups

Joining a useful useful resource institution is also a possible treatment method for a number of Antisocial Personality Disorder patients. Support groups provide patients a snug surroundings, wherein they may be more open to receiving advices and making modifications than in a greater formal setting. Patients can discover exceptional human beings in the ones organizations who higher recognize their ailment than those spherical them, and they could provide the affected man or woman with an impartial perspective in their cutting-edge conditions. The anonymity of the corporation offers the affected man or woman a shape of safety, at the equal time as the assist of the group offers them motivation to hold looking to enhance their situation. Moreover, the ones businesses additionally can be information hubs wherein sufferers can trade trusted information on property to be had for his or her conditions like an splendid psychologist from the community area or the side results of a specific drug. This is valuable statistics the affected character might not get keep of, or won't be willing to collect, from other venues.

The risks that consist of enterprise company remedy are present however oblique. Groups provide sufferers a platform, and even as this could be every releasing and beneficial, for humans with Antisocial Personality Disorder this will additionally gift danger. There is a opportunity that human beings might also furthermore be a part of those businesses to advantage have an effect on over others or a diploma in which they might enact their very own drama. These people are adverse to their treatments and to others, in preference to of help. Another disadvantage of manual organizations is that the group can be unsuited to handling the more complex troubles that Antisocial Personality Disorder gives. This is mainly proper if the patients Antisocial Personality Disorder is compounded through other troubles, together with despair or anxiety, which is probably each usually placed in human beings with this disorder.

Five.   Hospitalization

The maximum dramatic, and least critical, remedy opportunity for Antisocial Personality Disorder is hospitalization. Hospitalization of an individual with Antisocial Personality Disorder is quite unusual, and is normally handiest used even as humans have come into contact with the government. There are some times wherein humans are ordered thru way of the court to be hospitalized for their state of affairs in advance than, in some unspecified time in the future of or after court docket court cases as part of the penal manner. These people normally show excessive symptoms in their illness, and are in no manner the commonplace affected man or woman.

That said, hospitalization provide a few blessings as a remedy alternative. Individuals who're hospitalized can collect monitored care and may be appropriately identified through a expert. If distinctive problems exist along the Antisocial Personality Disorder, they're likely to be diagnosed with the aid of manner of the hospital's psychiatrist. The affected person may even accumulate the remedy they want-medicinal drugs or extended intervals of remedy. This is specifically beneficial if the affected person is going thru an intense episode, wherein hospitalization lets in the affected man or woman to rebalance his or herself.

There are principal shortcomings of hospitalization as a treatment opportunity for Antisocial Personality Disorder. The first of these shortcomings lies within the short-term nature of hospitalization. It isn't always feasible for a affected person to stay hospitalized for an extended term, in particular whilst their disease allows them to preserve a few stage of functionality. Hospitalization will now not frequently be extended beyond a few days, which poses a enormous trouble for the treatment of Antisocial Personality Disorder. Treatment that simplest lasts for a few days, no matter the truth that during depth, isn't possibly to supply extended-time period results for the ailment. Follow-usawith the useful useful resource of the medical institution or other care companies may additionally additionally growth the advantages received by manner of way of the sufferers from their hospitalization, but isn't always a probable prolonged-time period treatment approach.

Secondly, hospitalization is steeply-priced and is not feasible for plenty human beings. While court docket order hospitalization is free or usually so, opting to hospitalize oneself or a loved one is not. There is the possibility that the health insurance (if they're protected the least bit) of the man or woman is insufficient to pay for hospitalization and any greater prices want to be paid out of pocket. Not notable does this present a economic venture to the affected man or woman, it can also location stress at the own family and in the long term, might also furthermore ultimately exacerbate the affected character's state of affairs.

How to Choose the Right Therapy

Choosing the proper remedy for an man or woman is a touchy challenge that have to be considering the maximum seriousness. Every treatment desire has advantages and risks, and sufferers want to cautiously consider which possibility fantastic suits for their needs. It is likewise crucial for the affected individual to have a robust maintain near of his or her own situation in advance than deciding on a treatment desire. Antisocial Personality Disorder does now not continuously occur the same way in wonderful individuals, and the unique composition of the patient's illness must be taken into consideration when deciding on a remedy approach. This is in particular right because of the opportunity that other problems exists for the affected person further to their Antisocial Personality Disorder, and those separate issues can impact each the signs and signs the affected person displays, and the effectiveness of a treatment possibility.

For those motives, step one to selecting the proper therapy is to are attempting to find out expert recommendation. But this number one step might be to be a tough step for people with Antisocial Personality Disorder because of reasons like their dislike for authority figures and their problem in trusting others. To gift themselves to a professional and trusting that expert's judgment is a tough undertaking for humans with Antisocial Personality Disorder. However, that is a essential step for the affected person to triumph over their illness, and there may be no actual viable opportunity. Self-prognosis is a risky venture that runs the risk of missing wonderful troubles further to misdiagnosing the affected character's scenario. This can purpose the remedy of an incorrect illness, which could get worse the sickness that the affected person certainly has.

However, it's far comprehensible that those individuals need to have a few reservations on trusting some different's opinion on this form of important difficulty don't forget. It is unreasonable to anticipate an individual with a sickness to accept as actual with any other's opinion. Therefore, the affected man or woman want to take as many steps as feasible to construct their self warranty in their selected expert in advance than looking for a analysis. Researching the expert at the Internet, studying affected character evaluations, and asking about previous reviews treating patients with similar troubles are all steps a affected person have to take earlier than choosing their intellectual fitness care business enterprise.

Once a provider has been determined on and a analysis has been made, the affected character desires to drastically keep in thoughts his or her remedy alternatives. There are severa elements to take into account whilst deciding on a remedy choice and every of these elements will range according to person. For instance, a affected man or woman who has an infection that requires a treatment, which interacts poorly with serotonin inhibitors have to take into account if medicine is a probable treatment opportunity for him or her. Do his/her ailment effect their lives enough to justify taking a treatment that can have possibly excessive issue outcomes? On the alternative hand, are they willing to place in the try and spend the time to attain results with other treatment options? This is a query that the sufferers want to invite themselves while thinking about a therapy technique for Antisocial Personality Disorder.

To solution the ones crucial questions, the sufferers should conduct a studies. Information on remedies can be obtained thru the internet or at the neighborhood library for a higher assessment. Patients can also ask their doctors to offer them any records they'll have on the advantages and disadvantages of each remedy alternative. Most intellectual fitness professionals may have statistics on treatment options to be had at their offices and those who don't need at the way to directing the sufferers to the proper assets. Making a listing of the terrific and horrible factors of each treatment preference is a awesome tool to determine what remedy alternatives they'll be maximum inquisitive about pursuing and what now not to take.

Another crucial attention for those selecting a remedy for Antisocial Personality Disorder is the viability of the treatment steady with their personalities and lifestyles, taking as an example, a really busy human beings with out a excellent deal of time. Are the ones people going to contain themselves to informal remedy techniques like organization remedy? Will they bypass meetings or neglect approximately approximately 'homework' if you want to attention on brilliant responsibilities? If sufferers apprehend that that is probably the case, then what therapy technique could paintings amazing for them in region of organisation remedy? Would they be inclined and capable of do more formal remedy commands that they may agenda into their regular habitual? Or are they not inclined to dedicate a lot time to the remedy in their illness, and like to take remedy rather? Will remedy even assist them manage their sickness? These are the man or woman troubles that each affected individual should don't forget even as selecting an appropriate treatment technique for his or her sickness. Answering the ones questions and comparing their person times is an crucial trouble in choosing the proper treatment for an person.

In this applicable count quantity, likely the most important detail in selecting the right remedy is for the affected individual to invite and thoroughly keep in mind the opinion of others. It is important to are looking for the opinion of a highbrow health expert. Just as they will be capable of offering a reliable and sincere evaluation, they'll be additionally the remarkable deliver to find out what remedy strategies could artwork fantastic for the patient. A expert need to be knowledgeable about the viability of every remedy approach for their patients and so have at the manner to giving a dependable recommendation on remedy strategies. For instance, a expert want to recognize whether or not the prescription of drugs might gain the affected individual's conditions or not. However, professionals aren't the best sources who patients want to are in search of recommendation from. Family and friends are also valuable belongings even as making those essential options. These people are the closest to the affected man or woman and are normally extra able to identifying the affected character's strengths and weaknesses than the affected man or woman themselves.

These same humans most usually do not have something but the splendid intentions within the path of the affected character, and so can be trusted to be both sincere and nicely-inspired.

Once the patients have acquired their prognosis, considered their alternatives, researched the treatment options, considered the sensible application of the remedies, and sought the advice of these around them, they have got on the way to you decide on the appropriate remedy approach for his or her ailment. Patients ought to do not forget that remedies are not restrained to a unmarried technique and restoration methods that work best collectively with each other to maximise the results they get hold of from the treatment.

Chapter 6: How to Overcome Antisocial Personality Disorder

Overcoming Antisocial Personality Disorder is a frightening venture. This isn't an 'contamination' of the conventional type, which as quick as recognized and treated is 'cured'. Rather, Antisocial Personality Disorder is a state of affairs that a affected individual often want to battle along with his or her complete lifestyles. The capability to 'remedy' the contamination is restrained to treating the signs and symptoms thereof and some conduct alternate. Therefore, it is likely deceptive to say that an man or woman can 'overcome' their persona sickness. However, it's miles sincerely viable for an person to conquer the issues created through their illness and learn how to live a greater ordinary way of life. An person who has effectively determined out to understand his/her very own trouble and adapt, allowing to them to live a semi-everyday existence, has consequently conquer his/her Antisocial Personality Disorder. To accomplish this really worth purpose, there are 5 steps an man or woman desires to take.

Admit the Problem

The first step in overcoming Antisocial Personality Disorder is to understand and admit that a trouble exists within the first vicinity. This is a tough first step for human beings with Antisocial Personality Disorder, who've a difficult time seeing the effects of their horrible behavior for what they'll be. These human beings are every narcissistic and selfish, and those two mixed traits act to create a barrier for the affected person in recognizing their private culpability in horrible activities. Even in times for which nobody need to be blamed, the ones people aren't probable to take obligation for his or her non-public bad behavior or the effects thereof. They are more likely to shift blame to others, even when this is an irrational act. Their narcissism prevents them from seeing themselves as capable of growing a mistake, while their selfish thoughts-set concurrently reaffirms their proper to do as they please and offers them the phantasm that they will be the middle of everybody else's interest.

Breaking through those remarkable boundaries is a hard project. Patients are frequently not able to attain this on their very own, and yet resent being compelled to perform that through the use of others. This creates a paradoxical scenario that is regularly no longer resolved till or except a more formal device will become worried. When the ones structures (collectively with Child Services or the court docket docket tool) grow to be worried, they may probably pressure the patient to address their terrible behavior to break out from the effects. In those times, the affected individual is capable of admitting that they've a problem and they may be taking steps to address their disorder.

Seek Help from Others

The 2nd step in overcoming Antisocial Personality Disorder is to searching out help from others. A affected person with Antisocial

Personality Disorder isn't always able to making true improvement without the useful resource of others. The very nature in their sickness prevents them from doing so due to the reality the disorder every distorts the affected person's concept of reality and reaffirms their horrible behaviors. Moreover, often the affected individual may additionally want to have other issues at the facet of their Antisocial Personality Disorder that should additionally be handled and doing so with out the useful resource of others is clearly not feasible.

Seeking help from others refers no longer handiest to professional assist however to own family, buddies and business enterprise supporters as properly. While a professional is vital for the affected character to overcome his/her illness, it's far ultimately the ones surrounding the affected person on a daily foundation that has the quality impact on the affected man or woman, whether or now not or not that be an terrific component or not. Seeking out help from others and permitting them to understand that the affected individual has a disorder; a supportive can create a honest surrounding for the affected character. This first-rate environment can assist foster change inside the patient and lets in to alert the affected person and professional whilst the affected character is suffering with remedy.

Receive a Diagnosis

Receiving an dependable analysis of Antisocial Personality Disorder is each crucial and smart on the part of the affected person. The importance of one of these analysis cannot be overstated. Without a analysis, any remedy or remedy the affected person engages in is essentially a blind remedy. Each and anybody has a very precise set of conditions that results many one-of-a-kind components of his/her sickness, and ignoring those events to perform a self-diagnosis can result in a disaster. Moreover, there can be constantly the functionality that the affected person may not have Antisocial Personality Disorder however as an opportunity a aggregate of numerous problems.

Receiving an reliable diagnosis therefore works as a place to begin for treatment. Until the assessment is made, remedy can't begin. In fact, until the evaluation is made, available or appropriate remedy isn't always even appeared. Seeking a professional diagnosis is one of the essential steps to overcoming Antisocial Personality Disorder. A problem can't be without a doubt solved, notwithstanding everything, until it is been well identified.

Begin Treatment

The next important step, in overcoming Antisocial Personality Disorder is to start a remedy way. The to be had treatments and the elements a affected individual desires to bear in mind whilst selecting a treatment plan had been included formerly. However, the significance of starting treatment itself is some thing that need to likewise be addressed. Many humans with Antisocial

Personality Disorder do no longer see their situation as poor to themselves or others, within the occasion that they admit that they have got a situation at all. It is consequently common for those patients to avoid or ignore treatment options, believing that they may be first-rate or that they're able to make the critical adjustments themselves.

Whether immediately apparent or no longer, Antisocial Personality Disorder has a extreme, unfavorable effect on each the affected man or woman and those around them. This sickness can reason frequent, lengthy-lasting harm if now not addressed and have to now not be not noted through the affected person. Self-remedy is certainly not realistic, and need to no longer be considered as a viable remedy alternative. Changing ingrained behaviors and perception strategies, no longer to say in all likelihood treating chemical imbalances, is something that an man or woman cannot do on their very very personal. An out of doors supply must be present to act as a catalyst for trade and to decorate first-rate modifications after they get up.

Make a Concerted Effort to Change

It is sincerely authentic that patients with Antisocial Personality Disorder cannot trade with out the assist of others. It is likewise proper that the most essential factors for the achievement of overcoming Antisocial Personality Disorder are the patients themselves. While an outdoor pressure may additionally additionally act as a catalyst for trade and may provide every assist and incentives to alternate, the patients need to make the effort. No one need to sincerely stress every different man or woman to exchange if that character is unwilling to gain this. Therefore, the patients want to choice to regulate their behaviors, and war to accomplish that.

This isn't an smooth manner. Overcoming Antisocial Personality Disorder is a drawn-out method that, through the usage of using nature, consists of setbacks and barriers. A affected person who wavers in his or her conviction to deal with his/her disorder and make wonderful modifications can and will backslide in his/her development. Patients must be organized to make extreme, dramatic, and hard modifications to their very own behaviors and belief techniques in an strive to conquer their disease. Only then can they attain putting in place a terrific way of life that promotes each their welfare and of others.

Chapter 7: How to Find Your Escape

To get away from Antisocial Personality Disorder, someone need to first recognize what they will be escaping from. In the case of Antisocial Personality Disorder, sufferers want to interrupt out from their self-created realities. In this inner worldwide, the affected person sees herself or himself because the relevant determine, and this sunglasses his or her actions and perceptions within the actual worldwide. For instance, if the affected individual thinks of himself as a victim in his very very very own inner global, he's going to act due to the reality the sufferer inside the real international, regardless of whether he has been victimized or not. If the affected individual sees himself because the most effective essential man or woman in their inner international, he isn't always in all likelihood to care lots about others inside the out of doors worldwide. The discrepancies between those worlds sincerely create obstacles for the sufferers to triumph over and annoying situations for those spherical them inside the actual worldwide.

To get away from this internal global, sufferers have shape of options. For instance, patients might also moreover pick out to break out their inner global through consciously choosing to exercising their skills in empathy. As previously stated, humans with Antisocial Personality Disorder frequently lack empathy. The patients are not going to unconsciously empathize with a few other individual. However, by using way of deliberately increasing their viewpoints and consciously making an attempt to develop their empathy, the patients can also growth their natural empathic ranges on the same time as moreover escaping from their non-public worlds.

This, of path, is less complicated stated than finished. Utilizing an emotional tool that they are not proficient in is a hard venture and feeling an emotional impact may be past their skills after they begin this workout. In this situation, the patients need to try to make it an intellectual workout to place themselves in the minds of others, and to recognize the belief strategies and emotional states of others. Doing so, even even as in simple terms an intellectual pursuit; open the sufferers as lots as the arena of others, allowing them to get away from the false illusion that they may be the center determine in all realities. Eventually, this can allow the patients to interact their feelings, granting them an excellent more break out from their own minds and troubles into the psyche of each different man or woman.

If the affected person is unwilling or unable to interact in actively extending his/her empathy in the route of a few other man or woman, distinct feasible alternatives exist. For instance, in desire to focusing his/her empathy on a bodily character, the affected person may also choose to use literature or unique media to exercise his/her empathy. Books are important equipment as they allow the patient to gain a better facts of a few different person (even though they'll be excellent fictional characters) and observe situations through the standpoint of a person else. Patients who do no longer experience studying can also pick out to listen to audio books or can popularity on looking extra emotionally stimulating films or tv shows. Simply searching live movement performs also are proper strategies for the affected character to escape from their personal world even as studying an important socialization potential.

Another manner to interrupt out from this inner worldwide is to utilize meditation. Meditation is focused on re-centering oneself and expelling terrible mind and emotions. When a person achieves a truely meditative usa, his/her thoughts is 'smooth' through funneling out his/her terrible feelings. This does very essential topics for the sufferers of Antisocial Personality Disorder. First, this lets in the patient to relaxation from his/her internal talk that is maximum generally dominated with the aid of way of his/her very private troubles. This inner speak is risky, and is mostly a direct contributor to terrible conduct. Eliminating this terrible have an effect on for even quick periods of time may be a pleasant difficulty for the affected person.

Secondly, meditation offers the affected individual the capacity to calm their nerves and consider the options very well earlier than they may be made. For human beings with Antisocial Personality Disorder, rash, reckless and impulsive conduct is frequently the reason of loads in their troubles. Being able to prevent and assume earlier than making a decision and using the equipment taught to them thru meditation, allows the affected character to make calmer, greater rational selections. These options are lots a good deal less likely to have the bad results and might help the sufferers keep away from severe complications of their lives.

Developing wholesome, green interests is also a appropriate approach of escape for people with Antisocial Personality Disorder. The interest that the patients choose out need to be an interest that is each appealing and remarkable, and ought to provide the affected person the opportunity to attention mostly on subjects other than themselves. Knitting, sewing, mechanics, constructing and others are all viable alternatives for patients to pick out out as a appropriate approach of escaping from their ailment.

This is especially real if the affected person can use this interest to engage with others in a outstanding manner. For instance, a affected individual who chooses knitting as her (or his) interest can be in a function to make use of this skill for charitable functions. Knitting clothes for underprivileged kids, as an example gives double the benefit for the affected person. The first gain they attain from this interest is the opportunity to popularity on a project outside in their very very personal internal global, escaping from their troubles, doubts, and egocentric mindset.

The second advantage is acquired even as the affected person donates his/her try to those in need. Receiving the gratitude, thanks and emotional connection to the character they helped can be a fantastic effect at the affected individual. It can also assist the affected person installation an emotional link to some other person, which can be a decisive detail in treatment. If a real emotional connection is made with a person else, the affected person will normally price that connection due to its rarity. Feeling wished, capable and important to the individual that they have helped can assist set up an emotional bond to that individual, ensuing in lots of excessive exceptional impacts on the affected individual. In quick, with the aid of making use of their pursuits to perform charitable acts, patients can be capable of set up an emotional reference to others, thereby escaping from their personal internal worlds and overcoming, or at least lowering the consequences of their disorder.

Chapter 8: Schizoid Personality Disorder

Schizoid persona disease is a sample of indifference to social relationships, with a restrained collection of mental expression and revel in. Individuals with schizoid character disease not often revel in there may be a few element incorrect with them. The sickness manifests itself via early their man or woman years through social and mental detachments that prevent humans from having near relationships. Individuals with it are able to artwork in daily life, however will now not increase massive relationships with others. They are normally loners and might be liable to immoderate fantasizing and forming attachments to animals. They might do properly at singular jobs others might discover insufferable. There's proof suggesting the sickness shares an underlying genetic form with schizophrenia, and social withdrawal is a pleasant of each problems. Crucially, humans with schizoid person illness are in contact with reality, not just like the ones with schizophrenia or schizoaffective disorder.

Signs

According to the DSM-5, signs and symptoms of schizoid persona sickness embody the following:

Does not choice or enjoy close relationships

Appears aloof and separated

Stays faraway from social sports activities that contain massive contact with one-of-a-type human beings

Usually chooses singular sports activities

Little or no interest in sexual evaluations with any other man or woman

Lacks near relationships except with proper now loved ones

Indifferent to reward or complaint

Shows mental cold, detachment, or flattened have an effect on

Exhibitions little seen change in mood

Takes satisfaction in few, if any, sports activities

Causes

The purpose for man or woman conditions isn't appeared, but a extra hazard for schizoid man or woman ailment in households of these with illnesses at the schizophrenia spectrum suggests that there's genetic susceptibility to developing this illness.

Treatment

Little research has been completed on the remedy of schizoid personality disease. This is in component just due to the fact human beings with this analysis commonly do now not experience solitude or compete with or envy people who enjoy close to relationships.

Medications are not usually cautioned for schizoid person illness. Nevertheless, they will be in a few instances used for quick-term remedy of excessive anxiety states related to the illness. The presence of anxiety, generally delivered on by means of using way of fear of different humans, may additionally propose that a fitness prognosis of the related schizotypal person disorder is better right.

Individual treatment that successfully obtains an prolonged-term degree of take delivery of as right with may go, as it allows humans with the illness to set up proper relationships, in instances in which this is desired. Individual psychotherapy can slowly effect the formation of a actual relationship a number of the affected character and therapist.

Long-term psychiatric remedy is extra tough to pursue due to the fact this disorder is hard to ameliorate. Rather, remedy desires to pay interest on simple remedy desires to reduce contemporary pushing problems or stressors inside the person's existence. Cognitive-restructuring might possibly appertain to attend to fantastic types of clean, irrational mind which can be adversely affecting the patient's behavior. That restorative plan need to be certainly defined on the onset of treatment.

Chapter 9: Schizotypal Personality Disorder

Schizotypal man or woman sickness is an ingrained sample of questioning and conduct marked thru way of uncommon beliefs and fears, and trouble with forming and keeping relationships.

People with schizotypal person sickness are uncomfortable with close relationships and may show eccentric conduct. Speech may additionally encompass digressions, bizarre usage of phrases or show "magic thinking," like a notion in clairvoyance and regular fantasies. Patients usually enjoy distorted thinking and stay faraway from intimacy. They typically have few, if any, pals, and experience annoying around entire strangers in spite of the truth that they may wed and hold jobs. The sickness, which can also appear more regularly in men, ground areas via the use of early the person years and can exacerbate tension and depression.

Symptoms

People with this sickness live a long way from socializing and acquire little pride from speakme with others, a hallmark of the schizoid person too. Those with schizotypal individual, but, appear bizarre ideals (aliens, witchcraft, proudly owning a "intuition"). According to the DSM-five, the symptoms include:

Discomfort in social occasions

Odd ideals, goals or preoccupations

Odd conduct or look

Odd speech

Trouble making/maintaining friendships

Inappropriate display of feelings

Suspiciousness or fear

Causes

As with maximum person situations, the purpose for schizotypal person sickness is unknown, but there's an extended occurrence among family participants of these the scenario, similarly to the ones whose loved ones are at the schizophrenia spectrum. The prenatal chance factors that in reality study to schizophrenia also are pertinent to schizotypal character ailment, and that consists of maternal direct publicity to sure infections.

Drug use can be a contributing element for human beings already in threat of developing this ailment because of a hidden hereditary predisposition.

Treatment

Schizotypal patients now not frequently initiate treatment for his or her disorder, tending to search for treatment for depressive troubles as an alternative. There are those who might be helped via antipsychotic drugs, however remedy is most appropriate for max. Just because of the reality the developments of this disorder can't be essentially altered for those with moderate to excessive instances, remedy is commonly focused at supporting humans with this illness installation a nice singular existence.

Behavioral amendment, a cognitive-behavioral remedy method, can permit schizotypal person contamination sufferers to treatment some of their uncommon mind and behaviors. Acknowledging problems through searching movies and assembly with a therapist to enhance speech practices are reliable approaches of remedy.

Chapter 10: Schizophreniform Disorder

Schizophreniform sickness is a psychotic sickness recognized in any individual who indicates symptoms and signs of schizophrenia for the better a part of at the least one month however for much less than six months. If the signs keep for 6 months or greater, the prognosis is changed to schizophrenia or, in a few times, bipolar or schizoaffective disorder. Somebody with schizophreniform illness can't differentiate among what's actual and what is pictured to a point that impacts their concept manner, conduct, emotional expression, and interpersonal relationships. To meet the requirements for schizophreniform disease, the symptoms should now not be because of medicinal drug or leisure drugs, or to each different clinical or psychological problem.

Symptoms

According to the DSM-five, schizophreniform sickness can be identified if as a minimum of the following signs and signs and symptoms seem, and one of the 2 signs is deceptions, hallucinations or disorganized speech.

Delusions (thinking of that humans are speaking approximately you or spying on you).

Hallucinations (listening to or seeing things that do not exist).

Disorganized or ridiculous speech.

Strange or catatonic conduct.

Lack of fitness or loss of hobby in every day sports.

People with schizophreniform sickness typically withdraw from loved ones and keep away from social sports. Schizophreniform disease normally consequences in a lack of ordinary dwelling and social skills and big issues at university or paintings.

Like schizophrenia, schizophreniform disorder affects women and men in addition, but onset is normally earlier in men, typically appearing between the a long term of 18 and 24. In evaluation, start in women is extra not unusual among the ages of 24 and 35. It can be very important to are looking for evaluation and treatment as soon as severa critical signs and symptoms and symptoms and signs and symptoms appear, due to the fact the evaluation for a whole recovery is wonderful with early intervention.

Causes.

The reason of schizophreniform disorder is uncertain but might be related to genetics, abnormal mind form, or circuitry in regions that embody belief, and/or an environment or condition that begins offevolved symptoms and signs and symptoms in a person who's genetically willing to boom the sickness.

Poor interpersonal relationships or severe tension may want to probable activate signs and symptoms of schizophreniform inside the ones who are inclined. Children with parents affected by schizophrenia spectrum issues is probably at higher-than-common threat of growing the situation themselves.

Treatment.

Psychotherapy and antipsychotic medicinal capsules are the pillar of remedy for schizophreniform ailment, and are important to save you the development of schizophrenia.

Cognitive-behavioral remedy is normally used to help those on the schizophrenia spectrum recognize the infection and offer realistic strategies to control at the equal time as enhancing social and trouble-fixing talents. Other types of talk treatment that take a excessive fine approach can be similarly effective, as a minimum in the brief-time period. If violent or self-detrimental symptoms appear, hospitalization is probably critical. Family therapy can also assist cherished ones deal with the illness and have a examine powerful strategies to assist.

Chapter 11: Schizoaffective Disorder

Schizoaffective contamination is a believed illness that consists of each psychotic competencies (as visible in schizophrenia), and temper symptoms and signs and symptoms and signs that is probably both depressive or manic in dialogue. The psychotic and united states of the us of thoughts signs and symptoms and symptoms and signs might also occur together or at remarkable times. Schizoaffective disorder is identified in fewer humans than is schizophrenia: Approximately 1 percentage of the populace international may be diagnosed with schizophrenia; zero.3 percent with schizoaffective infection. Since the frequency of schizoaffective disorder is low and in reality as it's far composed of each country of thoughts and psychotic features, the disorder can be difficult to diagnose.

While at least 2 primary standards for schizophrenia want to exist, a crucial distinction is that people with schizoaffective illness are more realistic regarding self-care and of their functionality to have interaction with others.

Signs

In order to be recognized with schizoaffective disease, the DSM-5 specifies that at least 2 psychotic signs and symptoms and symptoms need to exist, and moreover country of mind symptoms and signs of a particular duration.

The symptoms and symptoms of psychosis (which correspond the number one standards for schizophrenia) encompass:

Hallucinations

Misconceptions

Chaotic questioning, speech, or conduct, which may also encompass catatonia

Flat have an effect on or anhedonia (so-called "terrible" signs of schizophrenia).

The state of thoughts symptoms that must exist consist of:.

Mania.

Racing mind.

Rapid speech.

Unusual or chance-taking behavior.

Depression.

Simply due to the reality the signs and signs and symptoms of schizoaffective ailment overlap with those of bipolar or depressive disorder and schizophrenia, the circumstance can be tough to recognize. Schizoaffective illness is diagnosed at the same time as there can be a time period with a top depressive or manic u . S . Of mind and, at the same time, at the least 2 psychotic symptoms and signs seem, or whilst there's no sign of a number one temper illness but easy signs and symptoms and signs and symptoms of schizophrenia/psychosis maintain for not less than weeks. While there might be time durations on the equal time as there are not any symptoms and signs of a country of mind illness, they exist most of the time.

Causes.

Although the cause is uncertain, genetics is idea to make a contribution in schizoaffective ailment. People with a parent or caretaker or sibling who has schizoaffective infection, schizophrenia, or bipolar sickness might be at better than commonplace threat for developing this example. The software program of psychoactive capsules and excessive or persistent tension might also additionally upload to begin for those who have an underlying predisposition to increase schizoaffective sickness.

Treatment.

Treatments for schizoaffective illness are just like remedies for schizophrenia. Antipsychotics are the mainstay of remedy. State of thoughts assisting tablets and antidepressants are regularly prescribed too. The illness can pass into remission at the same time as the proper medication is taken.

Chapter 12: Depressive Disorders

Depressive troubles are described thru relentless feelings of unhappiness and worthlessness and a lack of preference to take part in previously first-class sports sports. Depression isn't always a passing blue usa of the usa of mind, which almost each person research every so often, however a complex thoughts/frame health hassle that interferes with each day functioning. It now not fine darkens one's outlook, it's miles usually marked thru sleep issues and changes in strength stages and appetite. It alters the shape and feature of afferent neuron in order that it disrupts the way the mind techniques information and analyzes enjoy. Despite feelings of despondence and insignificance, despair is a fixable scenario. It may be dealt with with psychiatric treatment or treatment, or a combination of each.

Depression is a common scenario in modern-day lifestyles. According to the National Institutes of Health, every twelve months more than sixteen million adults inside the

United States enjoy no much less than one episode of maximum critical sadness. The possibility that a person will expand unhappiness in a few unspecified time within the future in lifestyles is type of 10 percent. Extended social tension and vital disruption of social ties are understood threat elements for depression, and great horrible lifestyles events along side lack of a loved one, or lack of a pastime, boom the following chance of sadness. Substantial trouble early in existence, like separation from dad and mom or caretakers or parental dismiss or abuse, may also produce vulnerability to top notch unhappiness later in existence via manner of putting the involved system to over-respond to pressure.

Definition

A depressive sickness is a circumstance that includes the frame, state of mind, and mind. It disables concept and hinders everyday functioning of each day lifestyles. It commonly triggers real ache each to the person experiencing the temper disruption and the ones that care approximately him or her.

A depressive sickness isn't the precise identical as a passing blue mood-- via definition, the symptoms want to be present for not a lot less than weeks. Nor is it an instance of private weak point or a situation that may be willed or wished away. Anxiety has an inclination to be episodic, with bouts lasting weeks or months. Though signs will be predisposed to remit spontaneously in time, some shape of treatment may be very important to reduce the probability of reoccurring episodes. Appropriate remedy can help many individuals who enjoy sadness.

Depressive situations are to be had precise workplace work, as holds actual with exceptional fitness issues which include coronary heart hassle. Three of the most not unusual kinds of depressive problems are defined right here. Nevertheless, all paperwork are marked thru version in the huge form of signs and their seriousness and staying electricity.

Significant depressive ailment, or large depression, appears in a continually depressing country of mind found with the aid of positive notable signs and symptoms and signs that interfere with the functionality to paintings, have a look at, sleep, devour, and experience as quick as fantastic sports. A disabling episode of sadness could possibly arise handiest as quickly as however more generally takes place severa instances in an entire life. Depression is greater than a condition best from the neck up. It additionally impacts the characteristic of many body structures. Scientists have installation, for instance, that immune function is generally jeopardized in depressive states, and impaired immune characteristic would possibly in element underlie the link of depression to such distinctive issues as coronary coronary heart problem.

Dysthymic illness, or relentless depressive sickness, moreover referred to as dysthymia, includes signs of sad or down nation of thoughts maximum days for nearly all the day over a long time (2 years or longer) however the depressed kingdom of thoughts isn't disabling, although it impairs functioning to 3 diploma. Many individuals with dysthymia additionally enjoy most critical depressive episodes at some time of their lives.

Some forms of depressive disorder contain minor model of abilties or growth underneath particular situations.

Premenstrual dysphoric illness manifests inside the week earlier than the begin of menses, subsides interior days after onset of menstruation, and remits inside the week after menstruation. According to the National Institutes of Health, three to eight percentage of ladies of procreative age meet strict requirements for premenstrual dysphoric disorder.

Significant disappointment with psychotic capabilities, or psychotic despair, occurs whilst a intense depressive fitness problem is discovered by means of manner of delusions and hallucinations, The psychotic capabilities is probably temper-congruent with the melancholy-- that is, normal with the depressive topics of personal inadequacy, guilt, nihilism, or death. Or the misconceptions and hallucinations can be mood-incongruent, no longer associated with such depressive topics.

Major unhappiness with postpartum begin, or postpartum melancholy, is identified if a lady develops a primary depressive episode within the direction of pregnancy or internal 4 weeks after shipping. It is predicted that three to six percent of ladies enjoy postpartum sadness.

Significant sadness with seasonal patterns, or seasonal affective sickness (SAD), is characterised thru way of the start of a depressive contamination at some point of unique times of the year. Typically, the melancholy develops in the direction of the cold weather, while there is confined natural daylight hours, and completely remits within the spring and summer season. In a minority of instances of primary melancholy with seasonal styles, the unhappiness takes place at some diploma within the summer time months. SAD can be efficiently dealt with with mild treatment, but nearly half of of those with SAD do not react to slight treatment alone. Antidepressant medicine and psychotherapy can lower UNFORTUNATE symptoms and signs, every on my own or in mixture with moderate treatment.

Signs

The following signs and signs and symptoms are catalogued through the usage of the DSM-five as signifiers of primary depressive contamination and at the least five need to exist in the course of the prolonged duration of low mood or lack of leisure in as fast as-thrilling pursuits. Not anyone reviews every symptom, nor do people revel in the exact equal signs to the exact equal diploma. Signs can also additionally range not only amongst human beings and but regularly inside the appropriate equal individual.

Relentless miserable, stressed, or empty country of thoughts most of the day, maximum days

Feelings of worthlessness or intense guilt

Loss of interest or enjoyment in sports which have been as fast as taken pride in, which incorporates sex

Consistent lack of strength or tiredness

Trouble thinking, concentrating, recalling, or making options

Sleeping troubles, morning awakening, or oversleeping (hypersomnia).

Significant alternate in urge for meals critical to unintentional weight reduction or weight benefit.

Observable psychomotor agitation or restlessness, or psychomotor slowing down.

Feelings of hopelessness or pessimism; reoccurring mind of demise or suicide, suicide efforts.

Causes.

There isn't any single motive for despair. Rather, proof shows it effects from a mixture of genetic, biologic, ecological, and highbrow factors.

Research freeing mind-imaging-- which embody magnetic resonance imaging (MRI)-- and certainly one of a kind upgrades suggests that the brains of humans who have depression appearance one in each of a type than the ones of humans without unhappiness. The additives of the mind liable for regulating country of mind, wondering, sleep, urge for meals, and conduct appear to feature surprisingly. But those adjustments do not disclose why the sadness has came about.

There are many pathways to depression. Genetic factors might also play a complex position in placing the quantity of sensitivity to positive sorts of sports activities, which includes but no longer restricted to the amount of nerve device reactivity to tension and other annoying conditions. Scientists understand there can be no unmarried gene worried: many genes probably play a bit detail in including to vulnerability; appearing collectively with environmental or various factors.

Though, unhappiness can take region in people without family histories of it additionally. There is giant proof that harsh early environments-- mainly studies of intense hassle like abuse or neglect in teenagers-- can create vulnerability to later melancholy with the useful resource of improving the sensitivity of the concerned tool to annoying or threatening activities.

Experiences of failure, rejection, social isolation, loss of a cherished one, or unhappiness or frustration in attaining courting or a few different existence objective normally precede an episode of disappointment. For that cause, many scientists regard the horrible temper kingdom of sadness as a painful sign that number one highbrow desires are not being met and that new techniques are needed. They moreover recommend that disappointment to a few diploma outcomes from a lack of abilities in processing bad feelings; some of the best remedies for unhappiness educate what can be considered crucial intellectual hygiene, cognitive and emotional device for managing horrible emotions. Trauma, that might crush emotional processing systems, is a few different typical cause for depressive episodes.

Depression in Women.

Females experience depression about times lots as men. Biological, existence technique, hormonal, and other elements-- together with experiential ones-- specific to women may be connected to their higher melancholy charge. Researchers have confirmed that hormonal dealers proper away have an effect on thoughts regions that effect feelings and country of mind, and they're further locating out how hormonal agent cycles can motive depressive states. Some women may be liable to the extreme form of premenstrual syndrome referred to as premenstrual dysphoric sickness (PMDD). Ladies also are liable to despair after giving shipping, whilst hormone and bodily changes, together with the brand new duty of searching after a helpless toddler can be anxious. Most women additionally uniquely face such examined continual stresses as balancing artwork and home duties, single being a figure, home abuse, and stressful for children and aging parents.

Ongoing research probes why some people confronted with large demanding situations expand depression, at the same time as others with similar issues do no longer.

Sadness in Men.

Countless men in the U.S. And anywhere in the worldwide additionally go through the psychic ache of depression. Research and scientific evidence establish that on the identical time as each women and men can amplify the number one signs of despair, they normally revel in disappointment in a unique way and may have one in each of a type methods of managing the signs and symptoms and signs and symptoms and signs and symptoms. Men is probably more glad to renowned tiredness, irritability, loss of hobby in paintings or pursuits, and sleep disturbances rather than feelings of sadness, insignificance, and excessive guilt. Some scientists query whether or not the same old definition of depression and the diagnostic assessments based totally upon it successfully capture the circumstance because it happens in men.

Depression also can have an effect on the bodily health in guys in a remarkable way from women. One take a look at shows that, notwithstanding the truth that melancholy is installation with an multiplied threat of coronary cardiovascular contamination in each women and men, simplest men revel in a raised dying fee.

Instead of acknowledging their feelings or seeking out assist in the form of right remedy, guys may likely flip to alcohol or drugs at the same time as they're distressed. They also can be mad, irritable, and, every so often, violently violent. Some men manage mental distress with the beneficial resource of throwing themselves compulsively into their work, trying to cover their disappointment from themselves, own family, and friends. Other men may additionally furthermore respond to despair with the aid of taking component in negligent conduct, taking threats, and placing themselves in damage's way.

More than four times as many guys as girls die by way of manner of using suicide within the U.S., despite the reality that women make greater suicide attempts at some point of their lives. In moderate of the research suggesting that suicide is generally related to sadness, the excessive suicide charge among guys may moreover display the fact that many men with despair do now not are searching for appropriate evaluation and treatment.

Encouragement and assist from involved own family members can be lifesaving. In the place of job, worker help programs or worksite mental fitness programs may be especially critical n helping guys recognize disappointment as a real illness that wishes treatment.

Sadness in the Elderly.

Contrary to three famous wondering, melancholy isn't always an regular accompaniment to getting old. On the other, older humans generally commonly have a tendency to enjoy growing up stages of achievement with their lives. Even so, while older grownups do increase despair, the situation might be not noted because of the fact it may seem lots less in emotions of sadness or sorrow and further in irritability or favored apathy or emotions of exhaustion. Also, melancholy has a tendency to have an impact on reminiscence, and within the senior depression can show up as confusion or troubles with hobby. Aging brings many life changes that can be triggers for sadness, which incorporates lack of a loved one, lack of employment and feel of motive, lack of effectiveness or appropriate health.

In addition, clinical conditions that arise greater frequently with age, together with coronary coronary heart ailment, stroke, and maximum cancers, may furthermore motive depressive signs and signs and symptoms and symptoms and symptoms. Or the drug treatments used for such conditions can also carry facet consequences that contribute to unhappiness.

There is a type of melancholy that develops in late existence, known as vascular depression, in some cases moreover known as arteriosclerotic unhappiness or subcortical ischemic disappointment. It arises from cerebrovascular damage that takes place with coronary coronary heart sickness. Brain-imaging research display that elements of blood vessel damage restrict blood go along with the glide to areas of the mind worried in feeling and u . S . A . Of thoughts law or to the thoughts's white rely. People who make bigger vascular disappointment typically have a information of excessive blood pressure, or hypertension. Vascular unhappiness could probably display up in worry, competitive inclinations, or lethargy and slowing down of motion. There are deficits in authorities function. Analysis may additionally furthermore include magnetic resonance imaging (MRI) to discover vascular pathology in specific additives of the thoughts. Vascular despair has a bent no longer to answer to antidepressant remedy; rather, the number one line of technique is probably varieties of psychosocial help and/or cognitive conduct remedy.

The majority of older adults with unhappiness enhance once they get hold of remedy with psychiatric remedy, antidepressant treatment, or a combination of the two. Research has proven that psychotherapy by myself may be effective in prolonging durations freed from depression.

Treatment.

Sadness, even inside the most extreme times, is a certainly curable infection. The quicker remedy starts offevolved, the extra powerful it's miles and the more the possibility that reoccurrence can be avoided.

Appropriate treatment for depression starts offevolved with a fitness exam via a scientific doctor. Certain drugs, and moreover a few health conditions, which consist of viral infections and thyroid sickness, can reason depression-like signs and need to be eliminated. Once a physical reason of sadness is disregarded, a intellectual exam can be completed, both with the useful aid of the examining scientific health practitioner or via referral to a intellectual health expert.

An assessment must include an in-intensity inquiry into the records and nature of present signs and previous episodes and their manage in addition to any family history of disappointment and its treatment. From this facts, the severity of present signs and symptoms and signs can be ranked; this information works as a elegant for measuring enhancement through the years and guides the course of remedy.

Once identified, disappointment can be treated with psychiatric remedy, remedy, or a mixture of each. Medication would probable assist lessen signs and signs and signs and symptoms and signs and symptoms on the identical time as psychiatric treatment addresses the bad mind, emotions, and beliefs that deliver upward push to distress and that need to be managed in greater green techniques.

Psychiatric treatment plans.

For mild to slight sadness, psychiatric treatment is commonly considered the superb treatment possibility. Psychiatric treatment is important in assisting clients broaden techniques for managing the situations that reason sadness and to correctly control the horrific mind and emotions that mark't he distress. Both cognitive-behavioral remedy (CBT), and interpersonal remedy (IPT) had been extensively tested and discovered to be green in treating melancholy. By training new techniques of thinking and behaving, CBT gives humans skills to deactivate horrible varieties of thinking and acting. IPT permits human beings recognise and art work through bothered personal relationships that could motive or intensify their sadness.

Research research have advised that for young adults, a aggregate of medication and psychiatric remedy can be the handiest method to coping with large melancholy and reducing the opportunity for recurrence. Likewise, a research have a observe taking a have a look at sadness treatment amongst older adults determined that customers who reacted to preliminary treatment of medication and IPT had been lots less possibly to have repeating sadness in the occasion that they endured their combination remedy for at least years.

Medications.

Antidepressants purpose unique neurochemicals-- drastically serotonin, norepinephrine, and dopamine-- diagnosed to be involved within the relay of alerts thru numerous thoughts circuits. Nonetheless, it is not truely easy how they artwork or why they're capable of take weeks or months to offer a quality impact-- the mind is a very complicated organ.

The maximum famous drug treatments are known as selective serotonin reuptake inhibitors (ssris). Ssris embody fluoxetine (Prozac), citalopram (Celexa), and sertraline (Zoloft), to name some. Serotonin and norepinephrine reuptake inhibitors (snris) are similar to ssris and embody venlafaxine (Effexor) and duloxetine (Cymbalta). Now in use for many years, ssris and snris coexist with older schooling of antidepressants: tricyclics-- named for their chemical shape-- and monoamine oxidase inhibitors (maois). The ssris and snris will be predisposed to have fewer sizeable poor effects than the older capsules. Still, drug treatments effect anyone in a few different way and there is nobody-size-suits-all remedy. Tricyclics and maois live important antidepressants. Finding a remedy software program program that works for any precise affected individual can also take trials of a couple of antidepressant and multiple type of antidepressant.

Antidepressants generally require time to artwork. Patients want to take ordinary dosages for at least three to 4 weeks earlier than they're in all likelihood to enjoy a entire recuperation impact and preserve taking the medication to preserve superior temper and to save you a relapse of the depression. Though antidepressants are not addiction-forming or addictive, rapid finishing an antidepressant remedy can reason withdrawal symptoms and signs or bring about a regression. Some people, inclusive of people with chronic or recurrent sadness, may additionally moreover want to live on the medicine indefinitely.

Despite the relative protection and reputation of ssris and other antidepressants, a few studies studies have recommended that they'll have unintended effects on a few people, mainly teens and young adults. The United States Fda calls for a "black container" caution label on all antidepressant tablets to alert the general public approximately the capability improved danger of self-unfavorable thinking or attempts in kids, children, and more youthful human beings taking antidepressants.

Adverse results can restrict the usefulness of ssris, snris, tricyclics, and MAO inhibitors. Many humans taking maois should observe full-size food and clinical limitations-- from white wine and cheese to decongestants-- to live away from probably immoderate interactions. Clients taking an MAO inhibitor should get a total list of confined food, drugs, and materials at the time of prescription. The most common terrible results of tricyclic antidepressants include dry mouth, irregularity, trouble emptying the bladder, sexual problems, blurred vision, lightheadedness, and daylight sleepiness. The maximum commonplace awful results linked with ssris and snris encompass headache, queasiness, tension and insomnia, agitation, ands reduced sexual choice.

The contemporary medicinal drug in the antidepressant toolbox is ketamine, an agent prolonged used securely as an anesthetic. In randomized, managed trials, a molecular version of ketamine, known as esketamine, has these days been determined stable and dependable as a treatment for unhappiness. Administered with the useful resource of nasal spray, it acts mainly unexpectedly to beautify temper. Further, research show that it additionally reduces suicidal wondering. It isn't completely clean how esketamine produces its antidepressant results, however the drug has a device of movement that is specific from a few other definitely available antidepressant drug. It binds to NMDA receptors in the mind, obstructing uptake of the excitatory neurotransmitter glutamate, which causes a fast growth in glutamate stages. The glutamate burst in the long run strengthens neural circuits in regions of the mind associated with perception, memory, and temper, stated to be impaired in sadness. The new drug, alternate-named Spravuto, is meant for grownups with remedy-resistant disappointment and, due to its potential for abuse, is run in medical specialists' workplaces.

Herbal Treatment.

Throughout the years, there was great interest in the software of herbs for the treatment of each sadness and tension. St. John's wort (Hypericum perforatum), frequently utilized in Europe, has excited hobby in the United States too, because it has been used for loads of years in masses of parents and herbal remedies. Certain current-day studies have tested the effectiveness of St. John's wort for despair.

According to the National Center for Complementary and Integrative Health, "St. John's wort isn't often inexperienced for unhappiness. Do now not use it to change traditional care or to hold off seeing your health care company." Farther, "St. John's wort limits the effectiveness of many prescription medicinal tablets. Integrating St. John's wort and effective antidepressants can bring about a likely dangerous decorate to your frame's degrees of serotonin, a chemical produced with the useful resource of nerve cells."

Neurostimulation Therapies.

Electroconvulsive remedy (ECT) is beneficial, especially for humans whose unhappiness is excessive or lifestyles threatening, or for people who can not take antidepressant treatment. ECT commonly works in times wherein antidepressant drug treatments do no longer offer sufficient remedy of signs and signs and symptoms. Over the previous couple of years, ECT has been a good deal superior. A muscle relaxant is given earlier than treatment, this is executed below brief anesthesia. Electrodes are placed at specific regions at the top to deliver electric impulses. The stimulation reasons a short (about 30 seconds) seizure in the thoughts. The man or woman receiving ECT does now not consciously experience the electric stimulus. For whole restorative advantage, at least a few classes of ECT, typically given on the fee of 3 weekly, are required.

Lifestyle Changes.

Research indicates that a few elements in every day living have a high first-class effect on kingdom of mind states. Those include a nutrient-wealthy healthy dietweight-reduction plan, exercising, direct exposure to sunlight and out of doors, and social hobby. Life style changes that deal with those factors are appreciably considered a wise direction in any treatment plan.

How to Help Yourself If You Are Depressed.

Depressive troubles ought to make an character feel tired, vain, helpless, and hopeless. Such terrible mind and emotions make human beings sense like quitting. It is essential to recognize that such terrible perspectives belong to the illness and generally do not replicate actual conditions. Negative mind-set fades as treatment begins offevolved offevolved to take effect. In the intervening time:.

Try to be with different humans and to talk in self perception to any individual; it is also better than being via the usage of your self and secretive.

Participate in sports activities that could make you experience better.

Even mild workout, going to a motion photograph or a ball endeavor, or taking element in spiritual, social, or other sports activities can help.

Expect your mood to enhance slowly; it takes time.

Because disappointment misshapes questioning, it's far encouraged to postpone vital alternatives until the despair lifts. Before choosing to make a extensive shift-- exchange jobs, get married or divorce-- speak it with others who understand you properly and feature a extra goal view of your scenario.

Let circle of relatives and friends help you.

How Family and Friends Can Help a Depressed Individual.

The most critical aspect everyone can do for a depressed individual is to assist him or her get a right evaluation and treatment. It may additionally want making a visit on their behalf and accompanying them to the medical expert. Encourage a cherished one to stay in treatment is available.

Psychological help is additionally important. This includes information, staying strength, love, and motivation. Engage the depressed person in verbal exchange and pay attention cautiously. Do now not disparage emotions uttered, however deliver an motive of truths and offer want. Do now not push aside remarks approximately suicide. Report them to the depressed individual's therapist. Welcome the depressed character for walks, getaways, to the movies, and unique sports activities activities. Keep trying. Though diversions and enterprise are needed, too many goals would probable boom emotions of failure. Remind your proper pal or relative that with time and remedy, the melancholy will convey.

Chapter 13: The Brief Psychotic Disorder

A quick psychotic ailment is an uncommon psychiatric circumstance defined with the aid of manner of unexpected and temporary durations of psychotic conduct, like delusions, hallucinations, and confusion. Signs can endure for only in the destiny or for as long as one month, however can be immoderate sufficient to region the person at improved threat of violent conduct or suicide. A bulk of times present for the first time whilst an man or woman is in their 20s or 30s, notwithstanding the fact that begin can take area at any age. Short psychotic sickness is differentiated from specific issues wherein psychosis occurs via its confined length, and it is not spark off thru drugs or alcoholic abuse. In many instances brief psychotic illness might not propose the presence of a persistent intellectual fitness scenario.

Signs

According to the DSM-five, signs and symptoms and signs and symptoms of short psychotic illness might probably include:

Misconceptions and hallucinations

Abrupt and extreme kingdom of thoughts adjustments

Ridiculous or disordered speech

Messy conduct

Catatonia

Women are more likely than men to increase quick psychotic ailment, especially postpartum. The DSM-5 classifies one subtype of quick psychotic sickness as psychosis with start inner one month of giving transport. The majority of folks who make bigger brief psychotic infection enjoy high-quality one episode and are able to resume all sports activities sports with out a eternal signs and symptoms or impairment. Many humans with brilliant man or woman conditions have a raised risk of experiencing a quick psychotic episode, as are those who've skilled harm or important strain. It is essential to recognize that the evaluation for brief psychotic sickness is generally proper. However, an initial psychotic episode can be the number one indication of a continual intellectual fitness scenario like schizoaffective illness, schizophrenia, or a country of mind disease with psychotic signs and signs and symptoms. The assessment of short psychotic sickness is typically reevaluated if signs persist for multiple month.

Causes

The reason for brief psychotic sickness is uncertain, however critical anxiety or harm-- which includes the loss of existence of a loved one, attack, or natural disaster-- can spark off an episode. Similar to extraordinary conditions at the psychotic spectrum, there can be a hereditary, biologic, environmental, or neurological basis for this episode. Neurological abnormalities had been decided in people with psychotic issues; some appear to be gift in advance than symptoms and signs and symptoms and signs and symptoms first seem, even as one-of-a-kind irregularities have been recorded after the onset of signs and symptoms. Brief psychotic sickness has a bent to run in families.

Treatment

Normally, a health or psychiatric professional will talk with the character to dismiss every other bodily or mental fitness circumstance that exists simultaneously or may be inflicting the symptoms and symptoms. Antipsychotic drug treatments and, if vital, antidepressants may be advocated to assist manipulate signs, and the person would probable actually need to be supervised constantly to make sure they do no longer damage themselves or others. Short-term psychiatric treatment can help someone understand and recover from brief psychotic sickness, control their capsules, and learn how to manage anxiety. The individuals who fail to look for remedy after a completely first psychotic episode are more likely to appearance a future reoccurrence of brief psychotic disorder or to ultimately be diagnosed with a persistent illness on the psychotic spectrum.

Chapter 14: Postpartum Disorder

Because of superb hormonal adjustments related to being pregnant and giving shipping, a few new mothers enjoy the onset of a depressive episode. While mild melancholy, or the "toddler blues," are genuinely not unusual, and can additionally reflect the residing fashion modifications accompanying new maternity, shape of 3 to six percent of women revel in the begin of a top depressive episode within the weeks or months following delivery. The episode is frequently decided thru the use of crucial tension or even panic assaults. In unusual times, the disappointment may be placed thru such psychotic skills as misconceptions and hallucinations. Professionals find out that really 1/2 of of of depressive episodes taken into consideration postpartum certainly have their beginning earlier than delivery-- known as sadness with peripartum start. Studies show that girls who enjoy temper and anxiety signs in the course of pregnancy are at advanced chance for growing a postpartum important depressive episode.

Signs

The mildest and most common form of postpartum despair is called the kid blues. Symptoms emerge spontaneously in some unspecified time within the destiny of the number one 10 days after childbirth, and commonly generally tend to top spherical 3 to five days. Although symptoms are distressing, they typically decrease within 24 to seventy hours. Typical signs and symptoms encompass tension, sadness, irritability, confusion, sobbing spells, sleep and cravings disruptions, and shortage of feeling for the kid.

Postpartum sadness can take vicinity any time within the first three hundred and sixty five days after childbirth-- normally inner 4 weeks after transport however in a few instances a few months later. Symptoms should exist for as a minimum 2 weeks and have to have an impact at the mom's capability to feature. Most sufferers revel in signs 6 months after onset.

Events that predispose a female to postpartum sadness encompass:

Previous postpartum unhappiness; one incidence also can increase the hazard of re-incidence by as much as 70 percentage

Depression unrelated to pregnancy; a previous episode may additionally additionally moreover boom the threat through 30 percent

Serious premenstrual syndrome

Stressful marital, own family, vocational, or financial conditions

Undesirable being pregnant or uncertainty about the pregnancy

Symptoms stated for postpartum disappointment encompass:

Depressed mood for nearly all the day and nearly each day

Loss of hobby in sports activities previously taken into consideration amusing

Despondence and despair

Thoughts of suicide and/or infanticide

Fear of negative the kid

Lack of mission or over-challenge for the toddler

Emotions of guilt, inadequacy, and insignificance

Poor recognition and impaired memory

Strange thoughts

Hallucinations

Terrible nightmares

Panic or tension attacks

Agitation or sleepiness

Postpartum psychosis takes location at a rate of 1 to 2 out of each 1,000 deliveries. Symptoms commonly take area in the first four weeks following delivery but can rise up whenever as a great deal as 90 days after delivery. It is recognized with the useful aid of a quick and extreme start. Women with this sickness are extensively impaired and war with deceptions and hallucinations-- from time to time with command hallucinations to kill the kid or delusions that the toddler is possessed-- and are in threat for suicide and/or infanticide.

Causes

While organic, psychosocial, and cultural components effect the condition, the exact motives of postpartum melancholy are unknown.

Hormonal agent degrees exchange appreciably at some stage in pregnancy, transport, and the postpartum duration. Researchers are reading a likely relationship among abrupt shifts in hormone ranges and postpartum melancholy.

Postpartum dysregulation of the thyroid gland can also furthermore contribute. The thyroid gland regulates a few hormones and manufacturing drops drastically after beginning, going decrease returned to commonplace functioning over a period of months. Thyroid modifications may additionally upload to the feelings of fatigue that newmothers normally enjoy.

Social and highbrow factors also can contribute to the start of a postpartum disorder.

New moms want excessive stages of beneficial aid of their new position, and extended postpartum unhappiness is connected to loss of social aid. New mothers want no longer only emotional guide but home aid, together with useful useful resource with home chores and infant care. Such help is probably missing for a single mother or for a lady with few members of the circle of relatives nearby.

Sleeplessness and tiredness are in truth commonplace proceedings following childbirth. Delivering taxes a female's strength, and it is able to take numerous weeks to get better. A cesarean transport is widespread surgical treatment and wishes even more recovery time. Integrated with the strength spent looking after a little one across the clock and tending to one in all a kind obligations, new moms nearly continuously experience insufficient relaxation. The resulting fatigue may additionally increase a woman's vulnerability and act as an delivered risk for depression.

The mom's converting position might also furthermore feed feelings of inadequacy.

A girl's attitude in the direction of her pregnancy may also have an effect on threat for peripartum or postpartum unhappiness. It is commonplace for a lady to feel doubt approximately being pregnant, particularly at the same time as unintentional. A higher occurrence of depression is stated amongst girls who've been ambivalent approximately being pregnant. Early lack of one's very own mother or a lousy mom-daughter dating can also reason a lady to sense unsure approximately her new infant. She may fear that searching after the kid will bring about ache, dissatisfaction, or loss.

Weight gain all through being pregnant also can have an effect on shallowness and growth the hazard of melancholy, as can breatfeeding issues.

Females who have their children by using way of cesarean shipping are likely to experience extra depressed and feature lower self-self belief than women who had spontaneous vaginal deliveries.

Moms with pre-term toddlers typically come to be depressed. An early start effects in unanticipated adjustments in regular and is an brought stressor.

A infant with a transport illness makes trade hundreds greater difficult for parents or caretakers.

The time period the mother spends inside the clinic may be associated with her emotional wellness. There's proof that early discharge will growth the danger of developing sadness.

151

The starting of a very first toddler is a specially demanding event for brand spanking new mothers and looks to have a greater relationship to depression than do the beginning of a 2nd or 0.33 teen.

Cross-cultural studies propose that the incidence of postpartum melancholy (but not psychosis) is a terrific deal lower in non-Western cultures. These cultures seem to provide the contemporary mom with a degree of emotional and bodily help this is particularly absent in Western society. In more conventional cultures, there can be greater reputation of the needs of motherhood. Thus, the new mother receives guarantee that the pain she's experiencing will bypass and that she may not need to address those emotions by myself.

Treatment

Postpartum depression is handled much like one-of-a-kind sorts of disappointment. The maximum common treatments for melancholy are psychotherapy, and participation in a useful aid system, antidepressant medicine, or a mixture of those remedies.

The maximum frequently used medicines to address sadness are selective serotonin reuptake inhibitors, or ssris.

As is the case with other medicinal capsules, antidepressants can discover their manner into breast milk. Women who breast-feed want to speak with their physicians to find out the most appropriate treatment.

Many types of psychiatric therapy, which incorporates some quick-term (10 to twenty week) remedies, can assist depressed human beings. Talk treatment options can assist clients get insight into and remedy their problems through communique with the therapist, at instances mixed with homework responsibilities among education. Behavioral therapists assist clients learn how to gather extra success and rewards through their private actions and a way to unlearn the behavioral styles that make a contribution to or rise up from their unhappiness. Furthermore, remedy can assist an man or woman recognise what triggers their signs and symptoms and signs, and the manner first-rate to address their distress.

Chapter 15: Borderline Personality Disorder

Borderline persona illness is a persistent situation that might embody temper instability, hassle with interpersonal relationships, and excessive costs of self-harm and suicidal behavior.

Borderline man or woman ailment (BPD) is recognized with the useful useful resource of time-venerated instability in moods, interpersonal relationships, self-image, and conduct. That instability regularly interferes with family and paintings life, prolonged-lasting planning, and a person's experience of identity.

People with BPD, to begin with idea to be at the "border" of psychosis and neurosis, war with troubles with feeling manage. While less widely recognized than schizophrenia or bipolar disorder, BPD affects 2 percent of adults. Many humans with BPD showcase excessive charges of self-injurious behavior, which include cutting and raised charges of tried and finished suicide. Problems from BPD and suicide hazard are first-rate in the younger-grownup years and will be predisposed to lower with age. BPD is greater common in ladies than in guys, with 75 percentage of times diagnosed amongst ladies.

People with borderline man or woman sickness regularly really need complete intellectual fitness offerings and account for 20 percentage of psychiatric hospitalizations. Yet, with assist, the majority stabilize and lead efficient lives.

Signs

According to the DSM-five, humans with BPD display a few or all the following signs and symptoms:

Efforts to avoid real or imagined desertion.

Intense bouts of anger, sadness, or anxiety that would last excellent hours or, at maximum, numerous days. Those is probably related to episodes of impulsive hostility, self-harm, and drug or alcoholic abuse.

Distortions in mind and enjoy of self can result in normal adjustments in prolonged-time period goals, career plans, jobs, friendships, identification, and values. At instances, human beings with BPD view themselves as essentially lousy or not worthy. They might also moreover moreover enjoy bored, empty, or unfairly misconstrued or maltreated, and that they have little idea who they are.

Reoccurring suicidal behavior.

Transient, pressure-related paranoid questioning, or dissociation (" dropping contact" with fact).

People with BPD usually have surprisingly unsteady styles of social relationships. While they could extend severe however moist attachments, their mindsets towards own family, pinnacle pals, and cherished ones may flow from idealization (superb appreciation and love) to devaluation (intense anger and dislike). Thus, they may form a right away attachment and idealize every different individual, but whilst a minor separation or dispute takes location, transfer all of sudden to the alternative extreme and angrily implicate the opportunity character of no longer being concerned for them the least bit.

The majority of human beings can tolerate the uncertainty of experiencing contradictory states at one time. Most human beings with BPD, even though, have to shift from side to side amongst right and lousy states. If they are in a horrible country, for instance, they have no recognition of the fine united states.

People with BPD are specially susceptible to rejection, reacting with anger and misery to mild separations. Even a vacation, a company enjoy, or an surprising change in techniques can spur horrible thoughts. These fears of desertion seem like associated with difficulties feeling mentally related to vital people at the same time as they'll be physically missing, leaving the man or woman with BPD feeling out of place or useless. Suicide threats and attempts can also moreover take region together with anger at perceived abandonment and dissatisfactions.

Causes

Although the purpose of BPD is unknown, each ecological and hereditary aspects are concept to play a function in inclining human beings to BPD. The infection is approximately five instances greater not unusual amongst people with close to natural own family individuals with BPD.

Studies display that many people with BPD file a records of abuse, forget about, or separation as youngsters. Forty to seventy one percentage of BPD clients report having truely been sexually mistreated, typically thru manner of a noncaregiver.

Researchers trust that BPD arises from a combination of man or woman vulnerability to environmental stress, neglect, or abuse as young kids, and a sequence of activities that trigger the onset of the disorder as teenagers. Adults with BPD also are substantially much more likely to be the patients of violence, which incorporates rape and unique criminal offenses. These activities could in all likelihood upward push up from destructive environments and the sufferers' impulsivity and poor judgment in selecting companions and way of lives.

Neuroscience is exposing brain mechanisms underlying the impulsivity, mood instability, aggressiveness, anger, and horrible emotion seen in BPD. Studies recommend that humans predisposed to spontaneous aggression have impaired law of the neural circuits that modify emotion. The mind's amygdala, a small almond-original shape, is a essential part of the circuit that manages poor emotion. In reaction to indicators from exclusive thoughts centers showing a perceived danger, it marshals worry and stimulation, which is probably extra noticeable below the have an effect on of hysteria or pills like alcohol. Areas in the the front of the mind, within the prefrontal cortex, act to dampen the interest of this circuit. Current thoughts-imaging research research show that character variations inside the capability to activate regions of the prefrontal cortex perception to be concerned in repressive hobby expect the capability to suppress terrible emotion.

Serotonin, norepinephrine, and acetylcholine are among the chemical messengers inside the ones circuits that make contributions inside the law of emotions, collectively with but no longer restricted to unhappiness, anger, tension, and irritability. Drugs that beautify mind serotonin function can also moreover beautify intellectual signs and symptoms and signs in BPD. Also, mood-stabilizing capsules which may be identified to boost the interest of GABA, the thoughts's large inhibitory neurotransmitter, may want to probable assist individuals who enjoy BPD-like mood swings. Such brain-primarily based weaknesses may be managed with help from behavioral interventions and medicinal drugs, a fantastic deal as human beings manage susceptibility to diabetes or excessive blood strain.

Treatment

The recommended treatment for BPD consists of psychiatric remedy, medicinal drug, and company, peer, and own family help. Group and character psychotherapy were demonstrated to be effective sorts of remedy for lots sufferers. Psychotherapy is the number one line remedy for BPD, and numerous types of treatment, like dialectical behavioral remedy (DBT), mentalization primarily based completely remedy (MBT), cognitive conduct treatment (CBT), and psychodynamic psychiatric treatment, had been studied and confirmed to be dependable methods to ease symptoms and signs and symptoms.

Pharmacological treatments are commonly encouraged primarily based mostly on unique aim signs proven by manner of the person affected individual. Antidepressant tablets and u . S . Of thoughts stabilizers may be useful for depressed and/or labile country of thoughts. Antipsychotic drugs also can be used at the same time as there are distortions in questioning.

Chapter 16: What Is A Narcissist?

Narcissists love themselves, the whole thing approximately themselves. Of route, there can be not anything incorrect with self-self perception and the notion which you are and are entitled to be the high-quality. A actual dose of self-love is essential to a pleasing outlook and healthy vanity. Narcissistic Personality Disorder goes similarly, it's miles a recognized intellectual man or woman sickness and signs and symptoms and signs and signs and symptoms and signs and symptoms can show as early as youngsters. It may be nearly impossible to deal with.

It is quite ordinary to be egocentric at times however humans with narcissistic character illness aren't handiest selfish, they will be additionally virtually missing in empathy or any functionality at all to endure in mind some other individual's issue of view. This lack of empathy method that a narcissist is able to pay attention in reality on their very very own pride with out feeling terrible for any horrific effect their pleasure may have on some other person.

Narcissists accept as right with that they'll be the very pleasant and consequently enjoy that others need to 'serve' them. Narcissists normally name for time, cash, attention and one of a kind topics from others without any consideration for his or her feelings and thoughts. If a narcissist husband wishes intercourse, he does no longer care that his accomplice is sick or too tired. He believes that sex is inner his proper to call for and he or she or he or he have to be venerated that he has demanded it from her.

Narcissists find out it very hard to countenance achievement or achievement in others. A brother had been given a selling at paintings? Don't have a very good time however due to the fact the narcissist will locate some manner to make the state of affairs about him. You observed out to pressure? You can also moreover additionally discover the narcissist claiming that the coverage is just too luxurious to permit you get proper of entry to to the own family automobile or the roads are too dangerous so as to pressure for your private with the children (in your very own safety and that of the youngsters of course!). Fundamentally, narcissists need to manipulate every element of lifestyles and they'll damage others within the event that they need to so that it will facilitate their non-public dreams.

On the ground, narcissists can appear extraordinary and fascinating, seductive even. This conduct is a part of their manipulate method. Narcissists recognize emotions and recognize the manner to manipulate them to their personal ends. They reel people in to their circle in advance than subtly starting to workout control. If a sufferer attempts to claim their very own authority the narcissist will respond and on occasion violently, subduing their sufferer to their will. Others will use emotions to blackmail their sufferer into feeling responsible for difficult the popularity quo.

Once the disaster is over the narcissist will shift all blame directly to the opportunity birthday party. Phrases together with 'have a look at what you made me do' or 'if you had not been so unreasonable, I could in no manner...' are common. Because narcissists are adept at handling feelings and are accurate at swaying people's perception, such behavior is often hidden. Many on the outdoor have no idea approximately what's taking place in a narcissistic dating or the quantity of control that the narcissistic associate is exercise over the opportunity.

Once a person has been reeled right proper into a narcissist's circle it can be very hard to break out. Strangely, the greater emotionally and socially literate someone is, the more difficult they might find out it as they can not accept as true with that they will probable be a 'sufferer'. Over time a narcissist will make bigger his manage, subtly setting apart their associate from all one-of-a-kind help networks. A narcissist boyfriend or husband is in all likelihood, for instance, to manufacture disputes or troubles with their partner's family. It is pretty common for a narcissist to file lower lower back on horrible reviews they have got heard family contributors express each approximately him or approximately their partner. The associate of a narcissist may be so used to idolizing him and believing his propaganda that they cannot possibly don't forget this man or woman is a bad have an impact on. Partners frequently protect the narcissist to their friends and family further separating themselves.

Once a narcissist has succeeded in taking someone a long manner from their help community they may be even much less complicated to control. It can take years for their victim to recognize that they're inside the manipulate of a narcissist and however extra time for them to pluck up the courage to do something about it. Many such human beings have been conditioned in some unspecified time in the future of the length of the relationship to believe that they could do now not a few element without the narcissist.

Chapter 17: How to Identify a Narcissist

In a dating wherein close to bonds can so effects cloud judgment, it may be very difficult to turn out to be aware about whether or not or now not or not you are residing with a narcissist. In this bankruptcy we listing some of the most critical signs and signs of narcissistic character illness. It is properly well worth taking the time to invite your self the questions proper right here and observe how they comply with to your partner and your house set up.

Narcissistic individual troubles can be present even in more youthful kids, certainly a self-targeted view of the area is certainly ordinary for infants and extra younger youngsters. As youngsters develop and broaden, their circle of relatives, instructors and different caregivers help mold their man or woman – showing them what is right and what is incorrect, training records and appreciation of others. Most youngsters bypass at once to make bigger a healthful arrogance. Others, however, keep to don't forget themselves to be the 'center of the universe'. Whether that is because of horrible parenting or due to an constructed in mechanism is arguable. Research has proven that the a part of the mind that offers with empathy is loads smaller in a narcissist than in someone who is not. If a infant with this thoughts shape is not then taught compassion, if he is idolized via his mother and father and given an unrealistic self-photo, if he isn't taught social conduct and popularity commands in teens, it's far highly probable that he is going to boom as a good deal as emerge as narcissistic.

Like many person issues, narcissism is a sliding scale. If your accomplice demonstrates extra than some of the tendencies indexed on this monetary ruin, then it is possibly that you are residing with a narcissist.

Does your associate have an inflated ego? People should be pleased with their achievements but in case your accomplice has an exaggerated revel in of his very very own importance it may be a warning sign. This is in particular so if he likes to exaggerate his gives at the rate of others.

Does your companion stay in a delusion? Most people have dreams and like to discuss them with their circle of relatives. Narcissists are specific, they frequently get hold of as proper with that the 'global owes them a dwelling', that they have to reap fulfillment in fact because of the fact they may be 'top notch'. If your companion idolizes her goals, if she believes in the fable of success and not the reality of tough artwork and competition, you can need to be worried.

Does your associate don't forget that he is better than others? Narcissists usually do not forget that they're past regular. They receive as actual with that they'll be too superb for everyday people to understand, that they're a person aside. As such narcissists often keep in mind that they belong inside the higher echelons of society, their career or any other relevant institution. Those who disagree with them are, of direction, too stupid to understand.

Does your associate enjoy entitled to crucial remedy? Narcissists typically be given as genuine with that because of the truth they will be so unique, they need to robotically be accorded preferential remedy – humans must be flattered that they'll be legal to do due to the truth the narcissist needs.

Does your associate want to be cherished? Narcissus, the legendary decide who gave his call to the flower and to this sickness, concept himself so lovely that he spent a whole lot of time admiring his mirrored image in a pool. Narcissists commonly have a propensity to have an exaggerated notion of their non-public beauty or professional success. They require the ones round them to affirm this superiority on a everyday foundation.

Does your associate use others? Narcissists will regularly haven't any qualms about the use of one-of-a-kind humans to in addition their very personal ends.

Does your partner have trouble know-how, or looking to understand the feelings of others? Narcissists are normally now not capable of empathize with the conditions wherein others find out themselves. They do now not grieve or have amusing with others but have a test how to turn some one-of-a-kind person's situation or feelings to their advantage. To this forestall, a narcissist will frequently have a awesome facts of the manner to govern emotions in others for his or her non-public ends but care little or no how such manipulation impacts everybody but himself.

Is your companion resentful? Because a narcissist feels that they're special, they're regularly unhappy even as one-of-a-type humans revel in fulfillment or positives of their non-public lives. Their fulfillment is, inside the mind of a narcissist, frequently unwarranted. She can also regularly agree with that particular humans are green with envy of her and her abilties.

Is your associate frequently haughty or immodest? Narcissists consider that they may be plenty higher than everybody else. For many narcissists, this could arise as a notion that they're able to deal with others with disdain.

The common difficulty taking walks thru most of these questions is a narcissist's agency perception of their very very own superiority and entitlement, coupled with an entire loss of empathy for the situations of others and any address their feelings. A narcissist can have interaction in any awful conduct from sexual abuse to robbery and experience clearly no remorse. Indeed many narcissists no longer most effective use the ones tools to govern others however experience the technique of manipulate – it feeds their perception in their very personal superiority.

Chapter 18: Living With A Narcissist

Is it possible to stay a satisfied lifestyles with a narcissist? Many humans decide that the narcissistic persona illness is an excessive amount of, that they can't stay with the manipulate their accomplice desires to exert over them, can not live with the rages and the located downs. However, in case you experience your relationship is worthwhile, and in case you want to, it is viable to live with a narcissist without losing your very private persona. It takes a whole lot of tough work but it could be finished. Ultimately, whether or not or no longer it's far actually worth persevering is a selection most effective you could make.

Of course you can pass down the easy course – you may allow your self to be controlled and denigrated. You can also want to reduce touch collectively with your circle of relatives and pals, pander on your narcissist's whims and permit them to determine how you live your lifestyles. This will skip some manner to avoiding warfare but on the equal time as this is possible inside the brief term, it isn't always specific for you, your vanity or for the narcissist. It is a essentially detrimental way of life and you deserve higher.

Many narcissists are, at a unconscious diploma, incredibly inclined. They are not aware about this vulnerability and their entire behavior is designed to save you others from knowing their flaws. To this end a narcissist will placed others down, manipulate them and feature immoderate reactions to any shape of criticism.

Knowing that someone behaves like this because they're subconsciously inclined does not lead them to any less difficult to live with. Even if you have recognized that your accomplice can be a narcissist, it can be exceedingly hard to get them to in reality take shipping of that there may be a few issue wrong with them and that they want help. Narcissists consider, greater than something else, inside the power and primacy of self. For this cause they're especially in all likelihood to reject any treatment as they may be incapable of accepting that there may be a few factor wrong with them. Even narcissists who've agreed to go to treatment have a propensity to take remarks very poorly. If feedback is given and given poorly, the destruction of the man or woman's center knowledge of who they may be can cause melancholy.

Even in case your narcissist will now not don't forget treatment for themselves, it is a fantastic concept for you to talk with a therapist. This will help you find out coping strategies for every day lifestyles and, likely most importantly, help you preserve a experience of your personal self confidence. Friends and family also can help in this – don't allow yourself to be remoted as this may increase the amount of manipulate your partner has over you and will in the end make you extra inclined. Indeed your help community is critical because of the fact you want to in no way anticipate to get any emotional resource from your narcissist. As we've have been given defined in in advance chapters, they'll be incapable of compassion and empathy and that they can't placed your worries first. You will need to get love and resource some other place.

Narcissists generally workout manage over humans the usage of 'FOG' a aggregate of worry, duty and guilt. This is a very effective cocktail of emotions and may depart the companion of a narcissist satisfied that every one the troubles in a courting are their fault. Narcissists will regularly manipulate their partners and youngsters thru rationing affection and hobby. This affection is withdrawn if the alternative individual stressful conditions the narcissist in any manner. In withdrawing the eye, the narcissist will make sure to location all of the blame on the opportunity individual – in the event that they had only behaved within the way he anticipated, he could no longer have had to be angry. A unique therapist will help you recognize the FOG technique and help you growth coping techniques to address it.

It is vital to set barriers – refuse to permit the narcissist (or others in tremendous) to manipulate you. Your time, your want and desires, your pursuits and your method are not a good buy lots much less important than every different man or woman's goals and also you do no longer constantly need to play 2d play around to anybody. Let him recognize what you're doing and be steady – if he manages to interrupt your remedy as speedy as, he is going to anticipate you aren't intense and agree with it is his right to interrupt it yet again. When you place your boundaries tell him that you may not take delivery of shouting and violent behavior. Let your narcissist recognize that you'll use a stock phrase – some problem along the lines of 'I am no longer going to speak on the equal time as you're angry. Come and talk if you have calmed down'. Then stroll out of the room.

This works because of the reality narcissists thrive on hobby. Sometimes the high-quality problem you could do is supply them vicinity.

If you don't allow your global to revolve spherical their concerns, it gets rid of, to a nice amount, the oxygen for their fireside.

Chapter 19: Narcissists As Parents

Narcissists now not first-rate have a terrible effect on their spouses and partners – they also can have a devastating effect on their youngsters. If you have got youngsters together with your narcissist partner, you'll need to be aware of the way to manual them as they arrive to terms with the relationship and its effect on their lives.

Narcissists are basically self-focused, and as such generally make lousy dad and mom. While they may be subtle enough an brilliant way to painting a extremely good photograph of a glad family to the outside international, their youngsters will regularly go through. The children of a narcissist parent are frequently decided for his or her love and affection and could do what they could to earn approval and love.

Narcissist parents regularly live lifestyles vicariously thru their youngsters, controlling their wishes and dreams. It isn't always untypical to discover the child of a narcissist following their parent's chosen career path or going to the college in their desire to make their determine thrilled with them. Such parents will regularly speak the kid's achievements down – not some thing is good enough. An instructional little one can be informed he's a failure due to the reality dad favored him to be well at baseball, a daughter that she is truely too unpleasant or that she is silly. The achievements are immaterial in the event that they do now not meet the narcissist's dreams. If they did meet the motive, it is considered an success of the narcissist's parenting in desire to the child's personal fulfillment.

Where a narcissist is the decide of or greater children, they may often institute a golden toddler/scapegoat dynamic many of the children. This dynamic lets in the discern to govern and control the siblings, placing distance among them and preventing them from appearing as a guide to every one-of-a-kind.

A golden infant can do no incorrect — their achievements are celebrated, their failures minimized. The narcissist parent will undertaking their self-belief onto this golden infant and make investments all their assets into making sure their success. A scapegoat, however can also additionally have their achievements dwindled and be rewarded (with a lessening of disapproval or some small quantity of affection) for screw ups. It isn't unusual for a scapegoat to be punished for achievement through a withdrawal of love or being prevented from continuing with a direction of have a take a look at or a interest which offers them pride and outcomes in success. A narcissist is incapable of fault and consequently any troubles inside the circle of relatives dynamic may be assigned because the responsibility of the scapegoat. The golden infant is encouraged to useful useful resource this narrative and it may fast turn out to be self-perpetuating.

While the scapegoat can appear to have the worst state of affairs growing up as all assets and affection are funneled inside the course of the golden infant, this changes because of the truth the kids mature and turn out to be independent. A scapegoat is used to independence, is used to locating their very very own manner. Their courting with their decide will almost honestly go away some intellectual scars and effect on all their future relationships, but they have got decided to turn out to be self-enough and to manage. A golden infant has grown up because the apple in their narcissist parent's eye. They feel entitled to everything and find it tough to live outside the glow of approval – they'll be at real chance of turning into narcissists themselves.